Insider Tips for Private Practice Startup Success

Harold Leonard, M.A., LPC-MHSP

CONTENTS

Introduction

Introduction

Starting a private practice was both an exciting and challenging experience for me. While it has been very rewarding, there were parts of it that frustrated me to the point of causing me to question whether I had made the right decision.

In the end, it was the right decision.

Before I get into the details of how you can successfully start a private practice for yourself, let me provide you with some background of my story. Even though everyone's path is a little different, my experiences should provide you with insights that will make your journey easier.

My Story

I completed graduate school in 1991 and have been a licensed counselor since then. Over the years, I worked in community mental health centers (four different locations for two separate companies) for the first few years of my career. Most of that felt gratifying, but my pay was at the lower end of the scale for our field, and the workload was heavy. Sometimes it felt like I was working at a factory instead of a counseling center. There was an emphasis on productivity and an expectation to see a certain number of unique individuals per month ("unique," meaning you had spread your services among different clients versus seeing the same client too frequently).

An opportunity arose for me to change jobs and work at an intensive outpatient program at a psychiatric hospital. This move was a career-changing experience for me, as I was able to work with very talented individuals as a team. We had one partial hospitalization group and two intensive outpatient groups and split them among four therapists. This interaction strengthened my therapeutic skills, and it provided more job satisfaction. I grew tremendously during this time. Unfortunately, the management of these programs was unstable, and there were frequent changes in programming and staffing.

I was eventually transferred to the inpatient side of the hospital. I had never desired to work in an inpatient setting, but it was a good experience for me. It allowed me to have hands-on training in addictions with more talented staff. I gained experience working with acute problems. The hospital later re-opened an outpatient treatment wing, and I went back to individual therapy at the hospital.

In the last year of my employment there, I was the outpatient manager. This position allowed me to learn the business side of therapy. I learned how to manage the budget, track statistics, and manage my team. I learned how to credential therapists and work with insurance companies. The hardest part for me was working with the large number of managers above me in the multi-hospital system. They valued the bottom line more than patient care, which bothered me. I fully understood it had to be operated in the black, as any business would. I am thankful for the chance I had to learn these skills, but I am equally thankful I no longer work in that corporate environment.

That position came to an end when we found out the psychiatric hospital was being closed. We discovered this on the local news while having lunch at a restaurant.

Losing my job unexpectedly caused me to panic a little but, I had two friends from the hospital that had gone into private practice when their jobs were cut earlier during a period of instability. They offered me to work with them as an independent contractor. I was scared and excited at the same time. I was concerned about not having insurance and retirement benefits. I knew it would take some time to get credentialed and build a clientele. Other options at that time were less appealing so, I took the chance.

I worked as an independent contractor in that office for thirteen years. I learned how to adapt to acquiring my own insurance and retirement plan. My friends provided the nurturing support I needed to succeed. I continued to learn about how to run a private practice. Our office was known in the community as a place to get quality care, specifically cognitive behavioral therapy.

As all good things must come to an end, one of the partners had to retire early due to health reasons. They had purchased the home in which the offices were located, rather than renting a space. They planned to sell the building as part of their retirement when the time came. The time came sooner than expected.

It was decided to sell the house and close the business. The remaining partner and I began the process of opening a new private practice. That journey, both the good and the bad, is the source of this book.

1 THE BEGINNING: BUSINESS IDEA AND PLANNING STAGE

So, you are considering going out on your own in private practice as a counselor or social worker. You may have gotten your feet wet by working your first job for someone else and decided you could do it independently. Or, you may have had the goal of going into private practice since you first chose to obtain a degree in the mental health field. Whatever the case may be, starting your own business can be a daunting task but rewarding as well.

You know how to do psychotherapy and are good at it. What you might not excel at is the business side of things. You may have taken a few business-related courses, such as accounting, but feel unprepared to open your own business.

Good news! You do not have to have an MBA to open your private practice! This book provides practical tips from someone who has been a clinician for over 30 years and has worked on both the provider and management sides of mental health. My effort at opening a private practice left me wishing there were more resources in one place to guide me through our journey.

What sets my book apart from other books and websites is I give you my insights into the process. I provide insider information and tips that other sources never mention. While researching my start-up private practice, the online information I needed to make informed decisions about the aspects of my project that were lacking in detail. All the websites had a brief description and little explanation of why one choice would be better than another. I am referring to all the stages of the process, from what business structure to choose, how to do accounting or taxes, and other pertinent pieces. These websites also were not designed to address the specific needs of the mental health field.

I spent a considerable amount of time researching and reading about it. You will save time since I have done most of that preparation work for you. You will also save a lot of headaches by being forewarned of potential pitfalls to look out for and by having a plan in place to deal with them if they occur. You should still read more about particular topics by doing your research in areas where you feel the weakest. This book will help guide you to good sources. I have included many start-up tips throughout the book to provide my insider information into potential problem areas.

I was reluctant for years to take the chance of going into private practice. My fears were holding me back. I was afraid of not being skilled enough to attract the number of clients I would need to be profitable. A sizeable marketing budget or extensive social connections to get enough referrals seemed necessary.

I was comfortable receiving an exact amount each month in pay in a salaried position and having benefits like retirement, things you will have to provide when self-employed. I was afraid of not making enough money and of losing the benefits I got by working for a company.

In the end, these fears were unfounded. I make as much money, sometimes even more, as I did while working for a company, but I get more control over things. Most companies have benefit packages offering paid time off, vacation and sick leave, and usually, some sort of retirement. I do have to pay for my health insurance and don't have vacation or paid time off, but I feel these trade-offs outweigh the downside of working for a company for me.

Most people do not like change. You, as a psychotherapist, are aware of that but know change is often good for us.

Opening a private practice is a bold choice but offers many rewards.

I want to make this decision easier by educating you on the process and providing insider knowledge of my journey in starting a private practice with a colleague. I am moderately skilled at planning, but I was unprepared for some of the events that took place. I have accomplished my goal if I can help you be prepared to start your own business. Your experience will undoubtedly be different, but there should be enough similarities to gain some insight.

I assume if you are reading this book, you are at least contemplating going into private practice, or you have thought about it enough to take the plunge. If you are still undecided whether or not private practice is for you, take some time to reflect on why you would want to go this route. What are the benefits for you and the potential costs? Why are you not satisfied with your current situation? Are you risk-averse?

As a stepping stone to going all in as a business owner, you might consider being an independent contractor and working in another provider's office. This setup provides the best of both worlds with limited responsibilities. It would require you to be licensed in your state and credentialed with insurance companies if you want to accept insurance, but not much more than that.

You would benefit from an already-established business providing you with referrals and the office support you need. For many, this might be all you need to fulfill your desire to be independent. Others may yearn for more. At least it would provide you with the experience and knowledge to go out on your own or help you decide it is not for you.

Becoming an independent contractor means you are self-employed. You contract with someone else to provide the office space and all the amenities you will need to operate as a therapist. You would sign an independent contractor agreement outlining the responsibilities of both parties, particularly financial matters. You would generally get a fixed rate of pay per client or pay a percentage of your income towards the expenses of running the business. Details of this approach are outlined later in the section on business types.

If you have decided to pursue a private practice or at least look into it in more depth, look at the roadmap in the appendix. It will help orient you to what to expect on your journey, giving you an overview of the process.

Creating and acting on your plan as you read through this text can be tempting. It is easy to become excited about the prospects and want to rush into action. I STRONGLY RECOMMEND YOU READ THE ENTIRE BOOK BEFORE TAKING ACTION, AS INSIGHTS ARE LISTED THROUGHOUT. TAKE NOTES AS YOU READ AND THINK OF APPLICABLE ITEMS. Reading and taking notes will help when you are ready to implement your plan. Obtain a notebook or use a digital one to develop your business plan. I used a combination of physical notebooks and folders to keep track of contact with insurance providers and a digital one to track progress and assignment of tasks. You will want to adjust the method to your needs.

Before we get into the details of starting a business, let me share my story so you have some context as you are reading.

Now that you know my story, it's time to get back to yours. First of all, let's take a look at the pros and cons of going into business for yourself.

Pros and Cons

Pros:

- You can decide the clientele with whom you want to work, whether it is adults, children, families, couples, trauma, addictions, etc. You will be more successful if you choose a particular niche. Many people wrongly assume they should appeal to everyone to fill their calendars. It is generally better to be known as the place that provides a particular service well than a place that just offers general services.

- You can set limits on how many hours you prefer to work and when and the number of clients you want to see. When working for an employer, you have little input on these things. You would have to recognize there are ongoing costs whether you work or not, and there would be a minimum amount of work you would have to do to cover them. This minimum is referred to as a break-even point, discussed later.

- You can choose your working hours and days without needing permission. Many people will like this perk. Those with small children at home, those who don't need to work full-time, and those who might want a hybrid of working part-time for someone and part-time in private practice would all benefit from this.

- You can leave the office and run errands whenever you are free. Some jobs permit this, but it is especially true when you are the boss.

- There is the possibility to earn more than when working with an agency. Your pay is limited by the employer, despite the workload increasing. Many agency employees are paid as salaried workers, so there is no opportunity to earn overtime pay. A person in private practice receiving $65 an hour from insurance and providing services to 30 clients per week (six clients a day) would gross $7,800 per month or $93,600 per year. Seeing four clients a day would equal $5,200 gross per month or $62,400.

- There is the freedom to make decisions about how the business operates, such as software choice, procedures and policies, etc. You would not be forced to use outdated software or fill out unnecessary forms. I have personally experienced this at more than one business. The software or forms often were developed by programmers without an understanding of the needs of a counselor.

- You do not have to complete employer-specific training and paperwork that make no sense to you. You will, of course, have to meet certain industry standards for insurance contracts and requirements as a business owner. You get to avoid all those awful corporate trainings you didn't want to attend if you worked for a large company. Every year I had to watch corporate videos about things like preventing sexual harassment and meeting accreditation standards and I had to keep current on CPR. Those aren't bad things to know, of course, but most of the time they were more annoying and repetitive than helpful. You will, of course, have to keep current on continuing education requirements for your degree.

- There is the potential for a sense of pride as a business owner. I am proud to be a business owner. By having more personal investment in the success of a business, you can feel satisfaction when things go well. Getting past the struggles can be rewarding too.

- You can change directions for the business and match the community's needs, such as meeting a need for more child and adolescent therapy; and more flexibility. If working for someone else, you are expected to follow their mission, vision, and values. As a small business owner, you can pivot much more quickly and make the changes you want to make.

Cons:

• There are no employment benefits, at least initially. You may have to get personal health insurance through the healthcare marketplace or a spouse, and you will have to obtain and pay for liability insurance. If you choose particular business structures like an S Corporation (S Corp for short), these costs can be part of doing business. Those costs would be pre-tax, which is what makes an S Corp desirable. Business types are discussed later.

• You may get lonely if you are the only provider; one of my friends was in private practice by herself for a year and decided it wasn't for her for that reason. Even though there are three of us in this office, we are still sometimes so busy we don't see each other frequently. Even if other providers are in the office, you may have less interaction with peers than if working in a larger organization.

• You might be personally liable for things if you are a sole proprietor or partner. This is the main reason we were looking at an LLC or S Corp. Personal liability can mean you can be sued and personally financially responsible in a lawsuit against your business. I am referring to your personal assets in addition to the business assets. An LLC or S Corp limits your personal legal liability.

• Some people prefer the comfort of being employed by someone else; owning a business does not allow you to just see clients and go home. You might not want the responsibility and stress of owning a business at this point in your life.

• You must learn about things outside of your degree: basic accounting, how insurance works, tax laws, etc. You may have to arrange for things such as networking computers, dealing with contractors, etc. I had to read and learn more about using QuickBooks, how the various business structures work, state and federal legal requirements, and other topics I previously did not need to know. I was not bothered by this but others may feel overwhelmed.

- It may require leadership and business skills if you have employees or independent contractors. These skills are not taught in psychology or social work schools. I believe all of these schools should offer a course on this topic as an elective.

- You only get paid when clients show up and/or insurance pays. If you take a vacation or miss work when you are sick, it will be without pay. The benefit of a salary at an agency is you get paid no matter what. This means you must realize your pay will vary from month to month and you might have to manage your personal (and business) finances more closely. I initially was concerned about this but adapted quickly. I have enough of a cushion in my bank accounts to ride the waves as my income varies.

- You will have to cover the operating expenses instead of your employer. Our expenses have typically run about 30%. If your gross income for the month was $5,000, your overhead or operating expenses would be roughly $1,500 (5000 x .30) if your expenses were similar to ours. Note: for a service business, this is called the COGS or cost of goods sold. In our case, it is the cost of services sold. This data can be useful in your financial planning, addressed later.

This list is not exhaustive but may give you some things to consider. I recommend adding your pros and cons to the list in the space below. If any cons concern you, stop now and work through the problem rather than telling yourself you will figure it out later. Try to resolve it or come up with a contingency plan before proceeding.

Pros:

Cons:

Starting the project

This tip is one of the most important. The process of starting a business involves many moving parts and numerous things you must track.

Keep notes on who is working on a project (like calling to get internet installed), who you contacted (name, phone number, and/or email address), the date you contacted them, details of the conversation (e.g., internet to be installed Friday, October 2nd between 1:00 and 4:00 and will cost $100) and any other pertinent information. This was especially important during the insurance credentialing part of opening our business.

Working on a small project can be difficult enough to track but, opening a private practice office consists of many small and large projects. If I had been working alone, it would have been challenging enough, but we needed to coordinate our efforts and communicate what had or had not been done. As mentioned in another section, we frequently thought a project had been completed only to find out later it hadn't.

We used two methods to keep track of progress. Kanbanflow.com is a website I highly recommend. Everyone in the office can access it because it is a website. You can access it from the office, at home, or on your phone. It also allows you to assign tasks to particular individuals so you aren't accidentally working on the same problem or, if you are, can see if someone has resolved it. It allows for notes, color-coding, and assignment of priority by placing items in a beginning phase, do today group, or a completed group.

It was very helpful to coordinate what needed to be done, and who was assigned the task and to keep track of where we were in the process. There were so many things to keep track of, and using this tool made it a breeze. I like the ability to coordinate with the other people on your team, no matter where they are or what they are doing. Assigning tasks helps to ensure you aren't both working on the same project or even worse, no one is addressing the task.

As a side note, it can be a useful tool to recommend to clients as well.

There is more than one variation of Kanban. I happen to like Kanbanflow as it integrates with your browser and is free. It keeps a running timeline of when you created and completed a task. For $5 per user per month, you get additional features but I found I didn't need them for my projects. I can see the benefit of the other features, however, and the price is very reasonable if you choose to go that route.

Another free option is Microsoft To Do. I was surprised at how useful it is. Some of the best features for me are how you can assign a date but also can choose not to, and how it can be attached to the taskbar at the bottom so it is an easy reminder to check my to-do list. I tried several other to-do lists and found them to be too complicated and not useful because of "features" like forcing me to give a task a due date. Sometimes the simplest option is the best.

Now you have thought about the pros and cons of starting a business and decided you want to do it; the next step is to create a business plan outlining your ideas in detail. Think of it like a blueprint for building a house. You wouldn't just start building a house without some sort of plan indicating where rooms, plumbing, and electricity would go. Likewise, it is inadvisable to start a business without a plan.

Start-up tips:

- Look at your pros and cons list. It is probably a mixture of positive and negative but don't let that keep you from opening your business unless there is a strong con. You might conclude it is something you want to pursue but the timing is not right.

- Starting a business is a large project needing coordinated effort amongst many people. Therefore, start right by getting organized with a system that works for you. Don't just depend on your memory.

Business Plan Creation

Creating a business plan is time-consuming but worth the effort, in my opinion. SCORE (Service Corp of Retired Executives) at www.score.org has many useful templates for creating a business plan, such as this one for a start-up business: Business Plan Template for a Startup Business. Search specifically for service business information. Because everything you might need is on this website, this book will not replicate the process. Even completing their one-page business plan is better than not planning at all, though it is worth the effort to do a full one. It doesn't need to be especially detailed unless you are seeking a bank loan.

One benefit of using the SCORE website is to identify your weaknesses and spend time understanding more about them. For example, my strength is in providing therapy but my weakness is understanding financial forms like profit and loss statements. SCORE provides numerous free webinars on these subjects and has a Start-Up Roadmap. Most websites focus on only one small aspect of the process but SCORE looks at the whole picture. Another website I like is www.bplans.com. There is one in particular for a psychotherapy center.

There are several things you want to consider for your business plan. The following are recommended sections and some questions to think about.

- Business: Define your business and its scope. What is your mission, vision, and values? Your mission is why your company exists, its main goal, how you are going to achieve that goal, and the reach of your company. The vision is what you hope your company will look like in the future. Your values are the company's priorities.

- Market analysis: Who do you want to serve? Who is your ideal client? Who do you not serve and why? What is your niche? From what distance will your clients come? How many potential clients are there in the area you plan to serve? NAMI (www.nami.org under "Mental Health by the Numbers") or your state's mental health statistics page can provide numbers to help you estimate.

- Competitive analysis: Who else in your community is serving the clients you want? How are they going about it? What could you learn from them and how could you differentiate yourself? Where will you locate your business to easily reach your clients? Complete a SWOT analysis, described later.

- Team management: Who will be involved in the business and what are their roles? What are their strengths and weaknesses?

- Description of services: What specific services will you provide? Do you take insurance or are you self-pay only? A new trend in the counseling business is to offer packages of services to clients. For example, you might offer 10 pre-paid sessions and include contact by text or email in between. You might even offer a discount on the 10-session package, charging for only 9 sessions as an incentive to prepay versus paying per visit. BetterHelp operates as a subscription service through recurring charges every week that you can cancel when you no longer want to receive counseling. Contacting clients by chat or text is a more recent change from traditional therapy.

- Marketing plan: How will you let potential clients know where you are located and what services you offer? Advertise where your clients will see you. How much will you spend on advertising? I have found little need for advertising beyond that which is needed for clients to know you exist and how to locate you. This is an area where you could easily overspend.

- Budget: How will you fund the start-up phase? How will you fund the first few months before you start receiving money? You want to begin thinking about a budget early on and start getting an idea of your expenses. The more data you clearly define, the better your plan will be. See the sample budget template.

- Financial projections: Create a sample budget as accurately as possible. Once you know the actual amount of particular items such as your monthly lease, insert them into your budget and adjust the numbers. Try to determine what your finances will look like at 3, 6, 9 and 12 months. Again, SCORE is an excellent source for templates and training on how to use them. Find them here: www.score.org.

SWOT Analysis

When starting a new business, developing a SWOT analysis of your business idea is highly advisable. SWOT stands for strengths, weaknesses, opportunities, and threats. The better you understand your business and your competitors, the better off you will be. As a counselor or social worker, the concept of competitiveness may seem like it doesn't apply but, we are talking about the business aspect of helping others.

When I set out to analyze my business idea, I started by outlining the geographic area from which I wanted to draw clients. Because I had already been in the business, I had a very good idea of where most of the clients came from. I looked at a spreadsheet of our client's zip codes and made a chart out of that. We were opening the new business just a mile or so away from the old one, so the data was useful for us.

Look up your competitors who are doing the same line of business you plan on doing; for example, outpatient mental health versus outpatient substance use disorders. Examine how they position themselves and promote themselves. Pay attention to what you think is effective and meets the needs of your community. There is an inadequate supply of therapists in most areas of the country at this time, but you may identify specific niches that can be met.

In my area, there is a need for applied behavioral analysts and autism specialists. You may not be sure what niche would work best for you, especially if you are just starting. In that case, you could see a variety of clients and get a better feel for what is right. Then, start narrowing down your clientele to fit the niche you like.

In our particular business, we specialize in cognitive behavioral therapy (CBT) and eye movement desensitization reprocessing (EMDR), two sought-after services. Little, if any, marketing needs to be done because clients seek us out. All we have to do is show we offer these services on online profiles or search engines.

In the strengths box, we could include several for our business. Our services are popular and clients actively seek them out and know about them. We have many years of experience and are credentialed in these areas, staying up-to-date through continuing education. We have built a good reputation in the community. Our secretary provides quick responses to emails and phone calls, answering questions clients may have and freeing the counselors up to see clients. We have heard clients complain that other counseling offices never called them back. What a sad statement for someone seeking help.

One of our weaknesses is that we don't specialize in some of the newer therapeutic models like ACT. We don't excel at substance abuse counseling, a service in high demand. Some have greater visibility through online media. We do not offer weekend services or late evening appointments. We have to provide for our own insurance and retirement. You probably will not have access to group insurance rates and will not have the advantage of a larger business paying a portion of your insurance costs.

Opportunities include reaching out to underserved populations and gaining training and skills in those areas. As of this writing, a casino has opened nearby. I have looked into the possibility of getting training specifically for gambling addiction in anticipation of the need. Because of our experience, we might provide training opportunities to others or create items to be distributed online. We could network more with other therapists. We have even considered branching out into satellite offices once our main office is firmly established. Another opportunity lies in the lessening of requirements for telehealth since the pandemic. We now can serve clients anywhere in the states in which we are licensed, not bound by the ability of the client to drive to our office.

Threats identified included the recent growth of counseling franchises and their appearance in our region. A similar thing has occurred with online counseling such as BetterHelp. These provide more access but could also cut into the bottom lines of local, small businesses. I have, however, talked with many clients who sought in-person counseling after unhappiness with online therapy. A threat or weakness in the industry you may not have thought about is how most insurance companies have not increased rates of pay for many years. Some of them have even declined. In a time where pay rates in most industries are increasing across the country and inflation has dramatically increased, this can be a net loss of income. Be sure to negotiate the highest rates you can get from insurance companies. You might not realize these can be negotiated.

Below is a SWOT analysis grid for your personal use. Put some time into thinking about your situation as you fill it out. You might consider doing one for the business idea and one for yourself as a therapist. If you are trying to decide between different ideas, complete one for each idea.

SWOT Analysis Example

Strengths:
- Many years of experience
- Good reputation in the community
- Centrally located
- Provide sought-after treatment modalities

Weaknesses:

- Only treat adults
- No weekend appointments

Opportunities:

- Gambling addiction training

Threats:

- New counseling franchises opening up in the area
- Online competition, such as BetterHelp

Your SWOT Analysis

Strengths:

Weaknesses:

Opportunities:

Threats:

Start-Up tips:

- You might not find this stage unnecessary or too much work. I find it worthwhile to think through a project as it helps me make more educated decisions later on.

- Consider doing a SWOT analysis on your business and yourself. What are your own strengths, weaknesses, opportunities for growth, and possible threats? Knowing yourself well will aid you in business. How does your business SWOT compare to your personal one?

Sample Business Plan

Let's create a SWOT analysis and a one-page business plan together.

Ashley graduated with a master's degree in counseling. She has worked for the past five years for a company providing in-home services for troubled youth. She likes working with children and youth but does not like having to travel over several counties, to be expected to fill out large amounts of paperwork on each client (usually at home after working out in the field all day), and having to work on weekends. She and her friend Jessica have talked about opening their own office.

Jessica met Ashley in college. She is employed at a community mental health center. She is expected to see a large number of clients and has no say in who she sees. Jessica is happy to have gotten a job straight out of school but it doesn't pay much. She also likes working with children but sees adults in her current position. She could transfer to a different position at her office when one opens up but it still pays at the lower end of the pay scale and, ultimately, would probably not be more satisfying.

Strengths: Both have several years of experience in providing counseling services. Both have the desire to work with children. The demand for counseling is high.

Weaknesses: Neither has owned a business. Neither knows much about accounting or finances. They don't want to work with adults, potentially turning away business (but they also know their niche).

Opportunities: They know there is a strong demand for individual and family therapy for children in their area. Many of their clients have complained about a lack of access to services. They could offer trauma-informed therapy that is not readily available from other providers in their area.

Threats: They would be competing with the already established organization Ashley works for. Other counselors in the area have more experience.

One Page Business Plan

- Business: Ashley and Jessica seek to open a private practice for underserved children and youth in their three-county region. They will provide individual and family therapy at times convenient to families. Their vision is to become known as the best place to receive these services. They value family, social connections, quality services, and supporting youth to become strong, independent individuals.

- Market analysis: They will serve children from ages 3 to 17 and their caregivers. The focus is on treating abuse and neglect to prevent this from becoming a generational problem. The clients will come from a three-county region. About 20 percent of the population in their area fits within that age range. Statistics show about 11% of that population have mental health issues.

- Competitive analysis: Both offices where Jessica and Ashley work serve these clients. They hope to offer more specialized services to complement these facilities. They decided to locate in the town nearest to the center of the three counties in which they serve, making it easily accessible to most of their families.

- Team management: Ashley and Jessica have decided to start an S Corp, with each of them owning 50% of the business (different business structures are explained later). They are co-owners and share equally in the decision-making. Ashley has more business knowledge and Jessica has more ideas about training they could get to differentiate themselves from competitors. They believe they would complement one another in business.

21

- Description of services: The business will operate by accepting insurance, Medicaid, and self-pay clients. They chose to accept Medicaid because they know many of their clients have it. They are considering a sliding fee scale for the self-pay clients. They will offer individual and family therapy, using their knowledge of DBT, trauma-focused CBT, and EMDR.

- Marketing plan: They plan on using word-of-mouth to let colleagues know about their new venture. They will both have a profile on Psychology Today. They will develop a website and advertise that on social media. They will also go to other offices that interact with children and youth and provide them with brochures and business cards.

- Budget: Because they have thought for a while about opening a business, they both have saved some money. Fortunately, both of their spouses are employed and supportive of their endeavors. They are gathering data to put into a sample budget to get an idea of how much their expenses will be each month and a general goal of an income they can expect. They are using the sample budget template found later in this book and understand some expenses are one-time costs of starting up. They have determined they are in a financial position to move forward with their business plan.

- Financial projections: They are using the startup budget to project the amount they expect to earn once they are on their feet. They are adjusting their budget as they go, inputting known data to make a more accurate prediction. They plan to work full time and expect to see about 25 clients each per week, grossing X amount of dollars. They plan, at some point, to add additional therapists once they are established.

One part of completing your business plan will be deciding how you want to organize it. Will it be a partnership or one of those things called an LLC? What's the difference? How do you choose? There are several options.

Choosing the business structure

Choosing a business type is something critical that will affect many other decisions you make later on. It is of utmost importance to spend some time educating yourself on the differences between these business structures. Once you are locked into a particular structure, it takes a lot more than just filling out a few forms to make changes. It is possible, but this change often affects many other aspects of the business. Unless you have a business degree, you most likely know little about the different structures. One frustrating problem is that many of the websites that describe the differences use the same, limited descriptions that only answer the most basic questions.

Most people are familiar with the sole proprietorship. Another option, partnerships, would be chosen if more than one owner is involved in operating the business. Other options include LLCs, LLPs, and corporations.

The complexity of the business types grows from sole proprietorship to corporation and you should consult with accountants and business attorneys to completely understand what is best for your situation. We spent considerable time and money consulting both before choosing S Corp as our business type. Everyone has different needs and different solutions may meet yours.

I found the website of the Forbes Tax Advisor to be especially helpful when I was initially learning about business ownership types.

For a clear explanation of the pros and cons of each type, Netsuite is a good resource.

To become more familiar with the tax obligation for each business type, you may want to look at LegalNature.

The following is a summary of each type of business structure, but I recommend you research the websites listed above for more detailed information.

Independent contractor:

You probably won't read about this option from most resources but, an independent contractor is one option to have more independence as a counselor. In this case, you are self-employed under a contract with someone else who already owns a business. This will usually be a small private practice already established. They provide the office space and amenities you will need; you show up and provide services. Your pay will be based on the contract you mutually agree on.

There are several benefits to this option. You have little liability to the business unless something is outlined in your contract. You might be liable if sued by a client (would need your own liability insurance or be included under the employer's policy). My contract stated I would provide a minimum dollar amount each month, regardless of income. This happened to be very small in my case. Then, I was contracted to pay a percentage for basically renting my space and using the resources. The remainder of the income was mine.

A great benefit for me when starting was I had a small amount I had to pay to the owners, allowing me to grow my clientele without losing a lot of money going towards my share of the expenses. The downside to a percentage contract was that as my income increased, I ended up paying significantly more as my income rose. As the income rises, the amount owed to the business rises. For example, many offices do a 50/50 or 60/40 split, with the independent contractor keeping the 60%. So, some simple math shows that if the owner keeps 40% of $1000, the contractor would owe $400. However, 40% of $5,000 is $2,000. Paying that amount per month would equal $24,000 a year going to the owner of the business. You might decide that is excessive or you may decide it is worth having limited responsibility. Remember this is not pure profit for the owner of the business; you are paying your share of the bills for running the business. This includes rent, utilities, office supplies, and all the other expenses. Ultimately, you would decide if the amount you are paying the owner is worth it or not.

My particular contract was to pay 35% towards expenses. As time passed and I learned more about running a private practice, this has seemed to be the average overhead, give or take a little, for operating in our area. This could vary greatly depending on the cost of rent and other expenses in the area where you will operate your business. One of the downsides is that as an independent contractor, you will have to keep up with estimated quarterly taxes and pay them online or face penalties.

I would recommend you try to negotiate a ceiling in your contract if you go the percentage route. The owner may not agree, seeing it as a way to increase their earnings. Get the contract upfront. Don't rely on a verbal agreement as memories can get fuzzy years later and miscommunication can happen. Most contracts generally use a flat rate per session. The business may decide to pay the therapist a flat rate of $50 per visit, no matter what the amount received.

There is a benefit to the owner of the business as well. The owner does not have to deal with hiring and firing employees, or set up payroll and deal with the state and federal requirements (taxes, forms, extra tax return duties) to do so. You might want to seriously consider this option to grow your private practice once you are up and running smoothly. The independent contractor would be responsible for paying income taxes and the owner would provide a form 1099-NEC.

Another benefit is you are not restricted to one office or company unless stated in your contract. You could work in different locations for different companies. I did this as an independent contractor and enjoyed being able to do various things throughout my career. This helped prevent burnout.

You may be isolated if you are used to working in a larger company with many employees and enjoy frequent interaction. To avoid this, become part of a local group that meets regularly for lunch or learning opportunities. If one doesn't exist, start one.

Another major downside is the lack of benefits - retirement, insurance, bonuses, vacation pay, sick pay, etc. I strongly suggest you set up some sort of automatic plan at the very beginning, even though finances may be tight, that will put back money towards these. Any small amount you can save towards these categories will not be missed as much if done automatically. As your income increases, increase the amount or percentage you are saving.

Sole Proprietor:

Sole proprietorships are the easiest to start because it is owned by just one individual who pays personal income tax on any profits earned. It usually doesn't involve more than obtaining a business license and paying local sales tax and quarterly taxes to the federal government. The major downside to this business type is the owner earns all the rewards but is also personally liable for any debts or legal judgments. You are automatically a sole proprietor if you go into a side business or project with the intent to make money, whether you declare yourself a business or not. You can hire employees with this option but may want to register a business name.

You will have to pay estimated self-employment taxes quarterly and be disciplined in setting money back for that purpose. Taxes are high because you are paying both employer and employee taxes. If you worked for another company in the past, they paid some of your taxes. Consider this option if you live in a state that has low or no earned income tax rates, as your taxes are part of your personal tax return. There is personal liability and you could lose your personal assets if sued. This is the most common small business setup because it requires very little to get started.

General partnership:

The second option to consider is a partnership. A partnership can consist of one or more individuals who want to share the profits of a business but also are liable for debts and legal liabilities. This operates the same as a sole proprietorship as it is easy to get started. You might want to register a business name and each individual will often pay personal taxes on the profits of the business passed through to them. It can be a good starting point but you may want to consider a more formal option, as each partner may be personally liable for the company.

A general partnership is helpful because you have more than one person involved in decision-making. It could be bad if you disagree, which will happen at some point. If go this route, be sure to have a detailed partnership agreement in the beginning so you plan how to handle problems before they occur, rather than disagree about them later.

You can find partnership templates online at websites such as www.rocketlawyer.com and www.lawdepot.com. Be aware that some of these sites advertise a free document but then require you to pay if you want to download it. This business type still has some personal liability. Taxes are passed through from the business to each partner, to be filed on their personal returns.

LLP:

A similar structure is called the limited liability partnership or LLP. This applies to certain occupations such as attorneys and physicians. Those professionals who I contacted felt that counselors, psychotherapists, and social workers would qualify for this designation. Partners cannot go after one another's assets to pay off company debts. Otherwise, the risks and benefits are similar to LLC. It may not be available in all states.

A limited liability partnership is relatively easy to set up and run but has some measures to protect personal liability. An LLP can be used to outline how partners come and go in the business, such as retirement or disability. It is sometimes used to handle sensitive situations; for example, when a partner may no longer be fit to practice in their field.

LLC:

One of the best ways to get around personal liability is to operate as a limited liability company or LLC. This limits personal liability but does require more paperwork filing with the state in which you live. There are annual filing requirements. Many people choose LLC as their form of business as it has a balance between lessening personal liability without excess documentation and reporting requirements of a corporation.

This business type is more common than an LLP. It offers personal liability protection and is fairly easy to set up and run. Taxes are passed through from the business to the individual, meaning the owner will pay taxes on their personal return.

Corporation:

The corporation is a formal business structure that sets up shareholders as owners of the company. The LLC, LLP, and partnerships can limit legal liability but the corporation is also separate from a taxation point of view. The corporation itself pays income taxes on profits that are not deductible business expenses. The corporation can even deduct employee salaries and benefits as part of its business expenses. The corporate tax rate is 21%.

It is taxed as a separate entity from the owners and requires much more paperwork and filing than previous business types discussed. A board should be formed and articles of incorporation should be filed with the state. Examples and templates of articles of incorporation are readily available online. Many of them claim to be free but then require a fee to use.

Stock is formally created, meaning you own a portion of that company. A shareholder, meaning they own stock in the business, will have to pay taxes on any dividends or distributions from the corporation. Taxes on the profit are paid by the corporation first and then again when dividends are distributed to the stockholders, who would pay on their personal income tax return. A S Corp, discussed next, avoids this double taxation.

Corporations can get investors in their business and grow as a company. This type allows business ownership to be easily transferred to someone else because they hold a portion of ownership in the business.

S Corporation:

A subtype of the corporation is the S Corporation or S Corp for short. This is not a separate business type but a tax subtype that allows tax breaks for the owners of the corporation. It is filed with the IRS as an S Corp and taxed accordingly. All the pros and cons of the corporation apply here.

We chose the S Corp for our business model. Before choosing which model works best for you, I recommend continuing to read the remainder of the book as it addresses some of the struggles we had with an S Corp.

The benefit of an S Corp is you pay taxes on what is considered a "reasonable" salary for your field. You can receive monies from the distribution portion of your business (the profits you have made) that are pre-tax dollars. This can be in the form of bonuses, payment of medical insurance, or any other benefits the corporation sees fit to provide to the owners.

According to nerdwallet.com, "Owners of unincorporated businesses are personally responsible for paying Social Security and Medicare taxes (collectively known as self-employment tax) on all net earnings from the business. Owners of corporations who are also employees pay taxes based only on their compensation." As an independent contractor, I paid these self-employment taxes. As the owner of an S Corp, I no longer have to pay self-employment taxes, since I am considered an employee of my own business.

Individual owners are taxed based on their salary and a portion is set aside as distribution to stockholders (that would be you and anyone else going into business with you in a small S Corp) when there is a profit. The stockholders/owners can take a percentage of distribution as pretax income but it should not be more than their salary as defined by industry standards. In other words, the government wants to ensure you are paying your fair share of taxes and take a reasonable (taxable) salary before distributing monies from profits.

If you choose to start a corporation or subtype S Corp, you are required to hold annual shareholder meetings (even though there may only be one or two owners) and elect a board of directors each year. You may also have to file an annual business report and pay a fee ($20 in my state).

I did not learn until three months in business that shareholder distributions in an S Corp must be less than your income or the overage will be charged a hefty capital gains tax. Fortunately, we did not take any distributions until the end of the first quarter since we were more focused on getting up and running. You have to be bringing income in to pay the bills before there can be any salary or distributions. We incorrectly assumed that in the fourth month, we could take money out of the distribution account to pay ourselves but the ratios were not good, resulting in the tax.

There are many companies online offering services to file S Corporation paperwork for you. They generally cost about $1500 and it is very tempting as most counselors and social workers know very little about business, especially corporations. We decided to hire a local accountant to file our S Corporation paperwork because it was someone we felt we had more access to if there were problems. We had mistakenly thought we had a verbal contract for this individual to be our accountant as well but found out later this was untrue.

After having looked at what we got for the money, most people could do it on their own and save lots of money. This is discussed in more detail below. There is also something to be said about the knowledge gained in doing it yourself. You understand better what is involved and how everything works together. For $1500, we got a few short documents filed with the state and a general S Corporation handbook. The documents themselves cost only $200 in our state to file. The handbook contained the articles of incorporation, by-laws, stock certificates, and templates for minutes.

Templates of these documents are readily available online, often for free. Someone with the knowledge of what is required can easily pull these documents together. I did not have that knowledge and understanding in the beginning and I have decided to share it with you so you can make an informed decision.

As for stocks, the proportion of ownership is determined at the onset of the creation of the articles of incorporation. For example, two counselors may decide to each have 50 percent ownership of the business. Stocks represent a fractional ownership of the company. When you open an S Corp, you print out stock with the name of your business, the stockholder's name, and number of shares owned. Technically, if there are two owners and one holds greater than 50% share of the business, they have the final say in all the decision-making in the business when it comes to voting at meetings.

Online Platforms:

Finally, I would be remiss in not mentioning the rapid growth in recent years of telehealth. Telehealth has provided tremendous opportunities for both clients and clinicians to provide better access. As with anything, there are pros and cons to this approach as well.

The more well-known telehealth companies include BetterHelp, TalkSpace, and Teladoc. These became very popular during the COVID pandemic as in-person clinics had to shut down their services temporarily. Some clients thrive with telehealth but many do not. VeryWellMind has a great review of these companies.

Clinicians who prefer online telehealth or have reasons why working from home may be more convenient may find working with one of these companies a better option than opening their practice. There are trade-offs, of course. Be sure to read reviews of what it is like to work for these companies as there are many negative ones. Pay is frequently vastly overstated. You may also have to be available at all times for some sites. In more recent news, I have read that some insurance companies are pulling back on paying for telehealth now that the pandemic is over. On a positive note, they do provide the clients and the workspace for you to do your job, freeing you from these tasks and expenses.

In Summary

As always, you want to consult with an accountant, tax attorney, or tax preparation business to get personal advice for your situation and to keep up with the latest tax changes. We were told that S Corporations used to be more advantageous than now, due to recent changes in law.

If you have any employees, you will have to pay federal and/or state unemployment taxes, although in some states you may not have to if you have only one or two employees. If you hire people as independent contractors, there would not be any unemployment taxes since you technically would not have any employees. The independent contractors would be responsible for their own taxes.

As you research information on business startups, you will discover many businesses exist to help you create your business. They offer to take care of the legal requirements, business formation, filing of paperwork, and other aspects of business startup. I did not choose to use any of these services but would consider them now that I know more about the process. I believe one can learn a lot by taking care of everything yourself but, if you are not inclined or do not have the time, these services could be helpful.

These online services are not necessary for forming a sole proprietorship or partnership. Their focus is on LLCs, corporations, S Corps, and non-profits.

Incfile.com is one of those options if you plan on opening an LLC, corporation, or S Corp. It has lots of clearly written, useful information on business formation and it can make filing easy. This website has a corporate kit you can purchase for only $99 as of this writing.

For my state, the cost ranged from $108 for basic filing to $407 for filing, templates, domain name and email, a bank account, and more. Looking back at the knowledge I have now, this is the route I would choose. We paid $600 for the same information from the accountant we consulted. I certainly feel it would have been worth our time to save $500 to do it through a website such as this. I do have to say, I cannot personally vouch for this company as I did not do business with them.

LegalZoom was recently voted the best overall business legal site by Forbes Advisor for 2023. You can find business documents, wills, business formation, and legal advice.

ZenBusiness starts at $49 plus state fees to file an S Corporation and $0 for other entities. It was voted best for business formation by Forbes Advisor in 2023.

According to Forbes Advisor, other sites to consider are as follows:

- Northwest Registered Agent: Best for Registered Agent Services. A registered agent is the individual responsible for receiving legal documents related to the business and relaying that information to the business. For our business, we simply named our secretary the person in charge of our documents.

- Rocket Lawyer: Best Membership Program. The membership program could be useful if you plan on seeking more legal advice in the future.

- Filenow: Best for Fast LLC Processing

Start-up Tips:

- Fully research your options and take plenty of time to decide what type of business you want to have. Think not only about the present but any possibilities of expansion later on, choosing the option that gives you the most flexibility. It is easier to do it the best way up front than to try and change it later.

- Ask others what business structure they chose and why. Ask if they have regrets and if they would make the same choices.

By this point in the process, you should have decided you are going into private practice, have done some research into how you will run your business, and chosen a business structure. You should have become familiar with a business plan and created either a full business plan or a one-page plan.

Now, let's get into a little more detail on the expenses of running a business. I had naively thought earlier on in my career that owning a counseling business would have minimal overhead. The product was my knowledge. I did not have to have a warehouse where I kept inventory of physical products I was selling. I knew the basics would be required - office space and some furniture - but had not put much thought into all the little things that could add up.

When creating a budget, you will be faced with making decisions on spending. Do I need brand-new furniture, computers, mobile phones, copiers, and faxes or can I get by with used equipment? It is convenient to sign up for an automated appointment reminder service but this monthly cost may not be worth it.

Expenses and break-even point

Making a proposed budget is one step in the business plan. It can be difficult to anticipate what expenses you may incur in a new business and even harder to gauge how much they will cost. Here are some ideas of areas to consider when developing your budget.

- Lease
- Utilities if not included in lease (water, telephone, mobile phone, sewage, trash pickup, electricity, internet)
- Electronic health record/billing
- Machine rental or subscriptions (copier, business mobile phone, credit card machines, fax)
- Advertising
- Office Supplies
- Software subscriptions (accounting, payroll, productivity software, email)
- Equipment purchases (PCs, copiers, fax machines, communications)
- Insurance (malpractice, rental, business liability)
- Payroll
- Maintenance
- Cleaning
- Security (alarm, backup software)
- Continuing education
- Reimbursement for license renewal
- Legal and accounting fees
- Taxes (business, income, property)

One of the things we have done at our office is to budget when certain items are due. For example, our annual malpractice insurance is due in September, two months after we started in business. Unfortunately, when starting a new business, you tend to start everything in the same month and recurring bills will happen in that same month. To spread out expenses, we have deliberately waited to start other expenses in a different month. That way, we can plan to have good cash flow and not run into problems.

We also took advantage of a few minor things to save some money. We changed from a monthly subscription for our billing service to an annual one and saved 15 percent on our bill. Because each of us is billed for that service separately, I switched mine over several months later so two annual fees are not coming out in the same month. As you build up your reserves, this won't matter as much but is a useful budgeting tool. If your finances are tight, you may have to keep a calendar of when these large expenses are due.

If you don't have a business degree or didn't take some basic business classes, understanding the break-even point may be difficult for you. It is worthwhile to think about when setting up your business.

A break-even calculation will make you consider the dollar amount of expenses you will incur, how much income you anticipate, and how many counseling visits you would need to break even. Break-even is the point at which your income and expenses are equal. You want to do better than breakeven but you need to be aware of the minimum.

A good online source that explains this is Service Business Break Even Analysis at Plan Projections. You will want to look for the section on service business for the formula to make sense, as a private practice is a service and not a traditional retail business that produces or sells a physical product.

You may want to download and use the breakeven calculator spreadsheet from the Plan Projections website to play around with the numbers. Another handy one is the business overhead cost calculator.

For our purposes, let's calculate the breakeven point of how many clients we would need to see. The formula is the breakeven number of clients = fixed costs / (selling price per unit - variable costs per unit).

Fixed costs are all the costs of doing business that do not change whether you see any clients or not. It would include salaries and wages, rent, utilities, etc. I initially thought it only meant costs that are always the same amount. Variable costs are all the other costs that may change depending on how many clients you see. For example, the more clients I see that pay by credit card, the higher my credit card fees would be each month. This would only count as a variable cost if you had no ongoing fees. You can look at monthly or annual fixed costs but be consistent with using both in your equation.

Let's plug some example data into our formula:

The breakeven number of clients each month = $3000 fixed costs monthly / ($120 per visit - $20 variable costs per visit) which would equal 30 clients each month to break even. If you receive an insurance rate of $65 per visit, the result would look more like this. Fixed costs of $3000 / $65 - $20 variable costs = 67 visits per month to break even.

These are imaginary numbers and are in no way meant to estimate how many clients you would need to see in your business. The more you can optimize your income and minimize your costs, the less pressure there will be to see enough clients to pay your bills. And, the more clinicians you have in your office, the better your ability to share expenses.

You can also use this formula to plan goals for your business. If you want to earn a higher income, use this formula to project how many clients you would need to see. If you have $5000 in fixed costs (including the desired increase in your income from the first example) / $65 - $20 shows you would need to see 111 clients per month, or 28 per week.

In our office, we would vary our take-home pay based on how much income we individually had for the month, minus half the expenses since there are two of us. We don't take a fixed salary and hope there are sufficient funds left to pay the bills. I suggest being conservative with your projections and happily surprised when you exceed them.

Once your business is up and running, the breakeven analysis should be recalculated using actual data versus the projected data you are inputting at this point. I found my projections were good for planning but you don't want to rely on this later.

Since we have been in business for over a year now, I used our first-year profit and loss statement to get the data to determine our fixed and variable costs, average gross income per visit, and other calculations. Once we have spent more time in operation and look back over 12 months, our budget should get clearer and more realistic. We will no longer be looking at the one-time charges for our start-up that would skew our figures.

Start-up tip:

• It can be tempting to just push the project forward and figure out expenses as you go along. I found there are often a lot more expenses than predicted. This can be both startup expenses and ongoing operating expenses.

Planning for the End?

Even though you are in the beginning stage of starting a business, it is advisable to think about your future and any problems or opportunities that may arise.

You probably have heard the saying, "Begin with the end in mind." This start-up tip comes from our situation where we were closing one office to open a new one and had purchased a book about how to effectively close an office. I recommend you purchase "Private Practice Preparedness" by Ann Marie Wheeler and Rob Reinhardt at the outset of starting your business because there are topics relevant to running your business.

In addition to retirement, the book covers what you need to do as a business in case of an emergency, disaster, illness, or death of one of the owners. Most of the time, no one likes to think of these things happening but being adequately prepared pays off. The book also includes very helpful, downloadable templates you can use in your practice.

I realized the advice and information were very applicable to our situation. If you set things up the correct way from the beginning, it will be much easier to handle changes later down the road. This might involve one of the owners moving on to another job, retiring, becoming ill for a long time, or other scenarios. If you plan ahead of time, there is less likelihood of misunderstandings or disagreements later.

This was one reason our attorney fees were slightly higher. We wanted to ensure we had included details about these potential occurrences in our startup documentation. I don't regret spending the time and money doing that, as it helped with my anxiety.

Start-up Tip:

- Consider how and when you might want to exit the business. No one likes to think about becoming ill or incapacitated but this happened to our colleague. She had to retire in her forties due to health issues, effectively ending the partnership. The plan had been for the partners to stay in business together until they both retired, presumably in their sixties. Consider how you would handle a situation like this. This is one reason we chose an S Corporation for the next business. One partner can easily leave and another partner inserted without closing the business. Technically, another partner could have been found for the partnership but it didn't work out that way.

My personality (INFJ on MBTI or enneagram 5) pushes me to do lots of research before making decisions about important things. My partner is a little more impulsive. We make a good team because of this. I can get mired in details and she helps me make the decision; whereas, I help her think things through more thoroughly.

I recommend you take the time to educate yourself in areas where you have weaknesses. In my case, I feel my strengths are knowledge and practice of psychology but my weaknesses are in accounting, managing a corporation, and taxes. I spent considerable time educating myself in the weak areas so I could ask informed questions when I spoke to professionals.

Name Choice

When choosing a name, you may also want to think about whether or not it has been taken online. Many of the potential names we chose were not in conflict with local or even state names but were taken by someone else at the internet level. States generally require you to pick a unique business name so it can be distinguished from other businesses. The state where I reside has a website where you can search for possible names to see if they are already taken. You can petition the state to accept a name that is similar but might be rejected and lose your filing fee, in addition to starting the process all over. The benefit of not having a name too close to another company is that your clients can find you easily and, if the name is easily remembered or found, will help market your new business.

Choose a name you like as it would be hard to change it later on, for many reasons. Clients will know you by the old name and may have trouble adjusting to a new one if you change. Changing your name with all the insurance companies and other businesses you work with would be very time-consuming.

Picking a name is also one of the first things you will need to do as your business name will have to go on every piece of paperwork filed. If you decide to be a sole proprietor, name choice doesn't matter. A business name and physical address are required for many documents. Some of them do not allow post office boxes.

Choosing a location for the business was not something I wanted to do early on because I was not ready to sign a lease that would require monthly payments without any income. We ended up using our old office address and later had to update everything. It made it easier to get started but then required extra work later. Ideally, we could have had a location picked out and not be expected to pay rent until we were ready to move in. We managed to do this with only one month without income.

One other thing that benefitted our particular situation was we were able to use a current landline telephone number for the new business and have it ported over to the new location once we moved. Potential clients were already familiar with and able to access the phone number. In your case, you may opt out of a landline telephone. We use a landline phone and supplement that with mobile phones or laptops for the therapists to use for telehealth video or phone calls. This has worked well for us. Be sure to use HIPAA-compliant websites of course. See the section on HIPAA-compliant resource recommendations.

Finally, if you provide a temporary address for your business, remember you will have to file a change of address with all the insurance companies, support services, post office, and other pertinent agencies. We moved from one location to another and had to ensure we contacted everyone involved to update our address. Some of the government offices were hard to recall but were very important to be included. You can't just depend on a change of address with the post office to inform everyone.

Start-up Tips:

- Brainstorm all variations of names. Ask others for input. We often came up with something we liked but others didn't, for reasons we had never thought of.

- Check the internet in general for your short list of names. Check website creation programs to see if a website with your name or an acceptable variation is available, even if you don't plan to have a business website right away. You might consider parking the domain name for future use.

- Check your state's business webpage to see if your name is available. They won't allow you to choose a name that would be confused with another business. This can give you some ideas for names, too.

2 THE MIDDLE STAGE: TAKING ACTION ON YOUR PLAN

In the first section, we looked at the planning stages of starting a business. Now, we will proceed to put that plan into action. Some of these steps will flow from the initial, middle, and into later stages of the development of your business.

In this chapter, we will look at legally setting up your business, choosing an accountant and possibly an attorney, getting the office up and running, and getting credentialed with insurance companies.

Tax preparer doing the business setup

Probably one of the earliest mistakes we made in the formation of our private practice was allowing our tax preparer to do our business setup. Choosing a tax preparer was one of the earliest choices we made, partly because we wanted some advice on what would be the optimal setup to allow us to keep the most income from our hard work.

The individual we chose was highly recommended by others and had a high profile in our community. It took several weeks to get an appointment, understandably since it was the end of tax return season. We felt good about our choice for tax preparation and she helped us feel confident about choosing the S Corp as a business structure. She explained to us that we were paying over 25% in taxes under a partnership and could save nearly 10-15% by choosing S Corp. It didn't take much discussion to convince us this was the way to go.

Because we had not educated ourselves enough, we didn't make an informed decision. She "sold" us the idea she could not only do our taxes but save us time by filing the documents to be an S Corp. Everything we would need would be given to us when complete. Once the paperwork was complete, we received a notebook with an outline and examples of the required documents for our new business.

Here are some numbers to give a better idea of the savings from an S Corp business type. The 2023 federal tax bracket for single filers making between $44,726 and $95,375 is $5,147 plus 22% of the amount over $44,725. If you live in a state with an income tax, which I do not, you would also owe that tax. You would pay anywhere from $0 in several states, and up to 13.30% in California, the highest state income tax rate (most counselors would fall in the 6-9% range in that state). So, 22% federal plus 9% California taxes would equal a 31% tax rate. Payroll taxes apply to sole proprietors and LLCs but for an S Corp owner, they are taxed only on the portion of their payroll. Any other money that comes from the distribution is not taxable. This is where the savings can come in.

Because we were in the process of closing one business while opening another, we had discussed how it would have been a good idea to have used an attorney to set up the old business initially. One reason this had not been done was because of the expense and also, not seeing the necessity as each business partner knew one another well. My business partner and I decided it might not hurt to have the attorney look at the S Corp documents to give us feedback. What we wanted to do was make sure it was set up correctly and future-proofed so that when one decided to leave the business, everything would be set up in advance to make it a smooth transition.

Our belief at the time was we needed an attorney to talk with us about future, long-term projections regarding business ownership. We were not clear that the attorney could help us set up the S Corp and provide the articles of incorporation that would meet our needs both initially and later. The accountant could provide the same services and the online companies discussed earlier are designed to do the same.

Unfortunately, this resulted in paying twice for the same thing. We not only had to pay the attorney to look at the documentation for accuracy, but we also ended up paying him to rewrite the S Corp documentation because the tax preparer had provided outdated information. It had references to laws that were no longer applicable or had been replaced with newer laws.

When we informed the tax preparer, we could not get a refund or return of some of our money and all the replies were short, not helpful, and had the impression of blowing us off. The tax preparer was not very accessible once paid. We later found out the tax preparer had not taken us on as tax clients after all. We did not discover this until tax time. They informed us they would not take on any more S Corp businesses at this point, even though they had set us up as an S Corp!

Needless to say, we were shocked. We approached this company with the proposal of them preparing our taxes. She offered to set up our business and we assumed, erroneously, that we were her tax clients since they took care of the incorporation. Thankfully, we had the foresight to check in on it before taxes were due. This new information explained why their office was so standoffish when we had questions. We had paid this person a significant amount of money with the expectation they would take care of both. We then found out that most tax preparers in our area were not willing to do taxes for S Corps because of recent, complicated tax changes.

Another major issue was we were told by the first accountant to start our business on July 1 so it would be a fiscal year for tax purposes versus a calendar year. What we were not told, and found out 10 months later, was that you are always a calendar year unless you file with the IRS to be on a fiscal year calendar. Even then, you have to have a reason for choosing a fiscal year. I did not discover this until the end of January, thinking I did not have to file taxes for the corporation until July, with a deadline in October. We would have been in trouble with the IRS had this not been discovered.

Start-up Tips:

- Ask others for recommendations. They have experience with the provider and can give you inside information on the pros and cons.

- Interview potential companies. It would be a good idea to narrow it down to two or three companies and meet with them to get a feel for how willing they are to spend time helping you get your business started. The difference between our first choice, which did not work out, and our second choice, was night and day. We needed someone to be accessible when we had the occasional question about setting things up correctly.

- Don't just go by online ratings. Our first choice had great ratings from others but we were very underwhelmed.

Attorney double-checked everything

Because we were unsure about how to set up our new business, we wanted to make sure we didn't make any mistakes. The previous partnership had gone relatively well but we had decided to proceed as an S Corp, unknown territory. Our tax preparer had offered to take care of all the setup and paperwork regarding the new corporation, but we wanted our attorney to also take a look at it. Unfortunately for us, this resulted in lots of extra expenses. He did uncover problems with the tax preparer's corporate paperwork, as it was based on outdated laws. In the long run, it probably would not have made much of a difference in how our business was run but we still wanted accurate information.

Doing this twice cost us at least an extra thousand dollars in legal expenses. We hope this pays off in the end, with us being able to dissolve the corporation or allow someone else to join with very few problems.

Spend some time educating yourself on types of attorneys and find one locally that specializes in business law. We were pleased with our choice.

Start-up Tip:

- Set limits on how much you allow the attorney to do. It can get very expensive quickly. Be very specific about what you want the attorney to do; e.g., scan your document for any legal issues and highlight them or create a whole document for you. We had our attorney look at documents created by the accountant and it led to research by the attorney on whether or not legal citations were up to date. The attorney did involve us in the process and had someone on staff conduct the research so it would be cheaper but, that wasn't something we foresaw from our initial request. It was more time-consuming and expensive than we had realized.

Everything costs, hidden costs

Something we have noticed in our private practice office is that all of the insurance companies have found ways to pass on the cost of doing business to the counselor or customer. One example is the growing use of digital credit cards as payments for services. While convenient and less expensive than mailing a physical check, the counselor now has to pay credit card fees directly out of their payment. Insurance contracts generally do not allow counselors to pass these costs directly on to the clients by charging more than the contracted rate. You are not allowed to do what is called balance billing, where you charge the client anything above the contracted rate for services.

Insurance companies have also begun saving lots of money by scaling back on live telephone support. It is nearly impossible to get through to a live person within a reasonable amount of time. I might have a 30-minute break where I could take care of some things but call wait times are often that long or longer. Insurance companies have even gotten to the point where they say the wait is long and then rudely hang up on you. A few more polite companies give the option to have a call back when the customer service representative is free but, again, if you only have a few minutes to wait, that option is not helpful. It also may prevent you from trying to make other phone calls out of fear of tying up the phone line.

Instead of costly human customer service representatives, you are now asked to search for your answer online or chat with someone. More often than not, I found that the answers online did not specifically address my issue or they were buried so deep you could never find them. To make the scavenger hunt even more challenging, insurance companies keep merging and/or changing names. Several times I discovered the information on the website, which I was told to follow, was outdated or just plain wrong. One insurance company said to just fill out an online form and send in a W-9 to update my information. Several months and multiple phone calls later, I discovered it was incorrect advice.

Another unexpected cost was payroll. In the previous partnership, we simply had the secretary write a business check once a month for wages but choosing to be an S Corp means you have to have a formal payroll and pay federal and state taxes. The cost started at $54 per month, an annual cost of $648 to write three checks a month. If you let an outside company handle payroll, they generally start at $150 per month.

You might also want to spend some time on training. Our secretary is awesome when it comes to customer service, scheduling, paying bills, balancing the checkbook, and other office details. She is less confident when it comes to QuickBooks. She knows the basics but it became complicated when we had to start payroll, which she had never done. We did find someone local who is a QuickBooks pro who helped us set up things the right way and answer our questions. It was money well spent. Do an online search for QuickBooks ProAdvisor to find local help.

By the way, if more than one person accesses accounts online, it would be wise to add those names to the accounts. I ran into this problem when we had to move payroll to a new computer when the old computer began having problems. Even though I answered all the questions correctly, QuickBooks could not help me because my name, even though I am an owner, was not the contact person on the account. I have to commend QuickBooks for protecting our data and privacy. I am more computer savvy than the secretary and thought I could take care of the issue while she was out, but it didn't work out that way.

Start-up Tip:

- Expect frustrations when dealing with insurance companies. It is just part of the business. Consider whether or not you even want to accept insurance in your practice. There are pros and cons. Keep detailed information about contacts, dates, what problem was solved, call-back numbers, and reference numbers. I kept these in a separate folder for each insurance company and had an ongoing to-do list in a notebook where I kept track of transactions.

Tax preparation for the partnership generally costs about $500-$600 each year for the business only (each partner filed individual taxes). We were shocked to find out that, not only was it difficult to find an accountant or tax office willing to do the taxes of an S Corporation, the cost ballooned to $2000. The promised savings of going the S Corporation route seemed empty.

After checking around, we were able to find someone willing to do the corporate taxes at $1900 plus individual tax returns at $400 each. I had always done my own taxes and generally paid under $100. This was another unexpected expense of an extra $300. Because of the complexity of tracking our share basis in the S Corp, we now are obligated to have the accountant do our individual taxes, making this an ongoing expense I had not anticipated. I was used to doing my taxes as an independent contractor.

A great deal of confusion for us arose around when to file our taxes. We had been led to believe by the first person with whom we worked, the tax preparer who filed the incorporation paperwork, that we had started our business on July 1 and our business was following a fiscal year instead of a calendar year. We later discovered we were not on a fiscal year. All S Corporations are on a calendar year unless you specifically fill out Form 2553 to request a fiscal year setup. Even then, the business has to explain why it needs a fiscal year setup versus the calendar year.

Another unexpected cost of having an S Corporation is the requirement to pay franchise and excise taxes in my state. That came to an additional $171 for our first year, which was only six months of business. A year after we had started our business and got the final bill for our tax return, we discovered another fee. After checking with the accountant for a more detailed explanation, we found out this was a one-time fee (in our state, anyway) for declaring we were exempt from needing a business license because we are a service/medical business. This was the accountant's fee for having to file an exemption from a state fee. Thankfully, that will be a one-time expense.

Start-up Tips:
- Create a budget based on information from this book.
- When making a budget, don't assume the charges will be the same as what you were paying on individual accounts.
- Be aware of the potential for unexpected costs.

Business fees are higher

Internet access in my area was $50 per month for the partnership because it was a personal account. When we started the business and switched to a business account, we were charged $95. Same company, the same internet, the same level of usage, and twice the fees. There was one difference - the business internet offered a business line of television channels. It just came as part of the bundle and it was cheaper to get that bundle than internet access alone. It was also just an introductory offer. We have never taken advantage of the television channels but could allow clients to watch television while waiting in our lobby. After the first year, it increased by another $40 per month. We called to get a better deal but none were available.

I had a personal cell phone that happened to bite the dust at the same time we were opening our business. My monthly charges were reasonable and I was generally happy with my service. I went to the local cell phone store to purchase a new phone. I happened to see an advertisement for business lines at $25 per month. Giddy with the excitement of starting my own business, I asked to add a business line so I could use my cell phone to make telehealth phone calls when necessary. Being the very gullible and/or unlucky person I am, I ended up with two phones. The individual at the store had told me, incorrectly, that I could not add a business line to the phone I had chosen and had already activated at that point. I wasn't happy with that plan but went along with it, seeing some value in having separate phones to keep my personal and business expenses separate. Once I picked out another phone and had it activated, he informed me my monthly fee would be $90, not $25. The fine print said you had to have five business lines to get the $25 rate. To top it off, I thought the more expensive phone was my personal one but the cheap phone I picked out for work had been set up as my personal phone.

Perhaps I should have asked a lot more questions but I thought we were on the same page in what I was seeking. He rectified the problem by switching out the cards. I came back the next day to cancel the business phone after thinking about it overnight. They took back the cheap phone and told me they canceled my business service but in actuality, canceled my personal service. I was then billed $90 monthly for a phone that had been shipped off to some unknown warehouse and was still active, even though it was no longer in my possession. They reactivated my new phone but required me to pay it off in full.

So, I now have a business phone that I use almost exclusively as a personal phone and can't deduct it as a business expense. My monthly charge is now twice what it was before I started. The upside is I have a new phone I like and it is paid for. I can now go to another mobile service provider if I want to but I am still traumatized and afraid of messing things up now they are working smoothly. Ironically, I get emails and postal mail begging me to come back - I never left!

Start-up Tips:

- Decide what business structure you want and then who will create it for you. You can save time, money, and frustration by paying someone to do it but you may decide to do it yourself if it is a simpler structure such as a general partnership.

- When creating a budget, don't just assume fees you pay personally will be the same for your business. Some charges will be higher.

- Consider all your options before switching items over to a business account.

Websites (and customer service reps) frequently have wrong information

When I first started looking into what needed to be done to open our business, like most people, I turned to the internet. The internet is a huge source of useful information for any topic, and there is plenty of information on business start-ups. What I didn't foresee, however, is how much information is outdated and just plain incorrect.

One particular insurance company has traditionally used its website for registering a client with employee assistance visits and, then, billing for visits once the client begins counseling. The website was outdated but served its purpose. It has an area to report any changes in network participation and changes with the provider. I naively updated this information, assuming that was all I needed to do to be in order. The website took the information and updated it but, I was no longer a participating provider after that. I was not informed and only found out when I went back later to work on a claim.

I figured a simple phone call to provider relations would straighten everything out. Dealing with insurance companies is seldom simple. I was told all I had to do was send in a new W-9 and a letter stating the changes that needed to be made. When I informed the customer service representative I had already done so on the website, she expressed surprise and was unaware of that being on the website. She stated she would inform her supervisor. Several months later, I noticed no changes. I sent the W-9 and letter at least four times without any change to my network participation status. Almost one year to the date of starting the process, I am now in-network but the website still incorrectly says I am not.

This is just one example of a website having incorrect or misleading information. I suggest you call multiple times to find out what needs to happen to become credentialed as you will many times get multiple answers. Each customer service representative would tell me it would take about 30 days for the paperwork to be approved. Initially, I waited 30 days to follow up, but later realized it cost me valuable time. I recommend you give it the initial 30 days but on subsequent calls, don't wait. I recognize it takes time to process the information through the company but don't assume it is going as expected.

In our current state of business in our economy, service representatives frequently change jobs, are often not trained adequately, are working from home without supervisory support, and most importantly, read from a script. If you ask a question not in sequence on their script, you will notice them scrambling to find the most appropriate canned answer. These answers are usually very frustrating because they are general and don't directly answer your question. I blame the insurance companies for this, not the customer service representatives. When we reached the end of the call, they would invariably, brightly ask how else they could be of service and if I was satisfied with their help. This was after I had received no help. I certainly don't want to do their job and understand they are doing what they were instructed. Their goal is to take care of the call as quickly and efficiently as possible, with a focus on productivity and not customer satisfaction.

An even more disturbing trend is to eliminate as many customer service representatives as possible. Don't be surprised to find you are chatting with AI and not an actual person. Who knows, maybe at this point the AI might be more likely to give a helpful and appropriate answer.

Another thing I have noticed is insurance companies often seem to bury information for providers. It is difficult to find the correct phone number and mailing address. Paying people to provide customer service is expensive. I understand everyone wants to cut expenses and be profitable. I have no issue with that. It seems to me, however, that they deliberately make it hard to talk to someone when the answers are not on the website. This is a common problem but customer service for actual consumers seems a little easier to obtain.

In today's world, many things about society seem to have changed. As a counselor, I frequently hear clients tell me they can't cope as well and are stressed by a society that seems broken. I believe this is due to several reasons. Training is not as good as it used to be. Job turnover in many industries has increased. Workers seem to be more entitled to higher wages while producing less work. Work ethics seem to have declined, with workers frequently missing work, calling in sick when they just don't feel like working, or "quietly quitting."

Start-up Tips:

- Don't assume the representative on the other end of the phone has the correct answers. You will pick up that they are reading from a script and if there is something they are unsure of, answers will sound like a script. You might want to ask to be sent up the line to a supervisor or call back to get a different representative.

- Follow up frequently because the likelihood there is a problem will probably not be picked up by the insurance company. Do not assume they have access to all the tracking information.

Early Financing

When opening our new business, we expected to use our savings and some supplies we already had. We wanted to open a business credit card to establish a line of credit for the business and to charge things directly to the business instead of using our own funds or being reimbursed later. After choosing a credit union for banking, we approached them to obtain a credit card. What we had not anticipated was that, because we were a new startup, there was no credit history. We argued we had been in private practice for years and were solvent. One of the partners even had an account with the credit union. We were asked to fill out paperwork that was the equivalent of taking out a mortgage. Instead of taking the time to do this, a personal credit card was opened to use until the business was in operation for at least a year and could convert that card or open a different business account. As of this writing, it is too soon to tell whether we will convert the one we have or open a new business card.

We, fortunately, did not need a loan to start our business. I imagine it would have been difficult to obtain a loan for the same reasons outlined above. It probably would have required a business plan and willingness to put up personal collateral.

Start-up Tip:

- Don't expect to get a credit card for a business that does not yet exist. It may have to be based on your personal credit. Be diligent about paying at the least the minimum so as not to damage your personal credit score. My credit score took a hit when I got our business card but recovered once good credit was established on that account. The decrease happened simply because I had access to more credit, not because we weren't paying the bills.

Credentialing

Starting insurance panels early

First of all, it is important to think about whether or not you even want to accept insurance in your private practice. Many providers have chosen to go the non-insurance route and have thriving practices. The reasons for this change are many. It is difficult to maneuver the process of getting on insurance panels. It is harder to find a live person to ask questions directly and it takes sometimes months to be approved. As mentioned in another section, you will often get conflicting information from the companies and will have to keep trying until all the kinks are worked out. Many clients do not want their issues flagged by an insurance company and used against them later, citing privacy as their main concern.

Other clients have insurance but find it difficult to find a provider, particularly in a smaller town. This is especially true in my area with Medicare. Medicare is notoriously hard to deal with and many providers just choose to avoid the hassle. We often get calls from clients who just became eligible for Medicare and are excited because they think they can get more services for free or a reduced rate, only to find out very few providers take it. If you decide not to take insurance, call around and see what the going rates are for out-of-pocket pay and price yourself accordingly. Medicare has been paying higher amounts to providers more recently but this seems to fluctuate.

A reason to accept insurance is many clients will want to use it if they can. They are paying for it and want to benefit from it if possible. Some may have met their deductibles and would have to pay little, if anything, out of pocket. A downside is you are restricted to the amount in your contract with the insurance company. Contracts state you cannot balance bill your clients. In other words, you can't ask for more than the contracted rate to make up the difference between what insurance allows and what you charge.

If you have decided you do want to take insurance, which our office does, expect several months of back-and-forth phone calls, emails, and delays. Start getting on all the panels as early as possible. You will often be told it will take 30 business days to be approved. If you call before that time, you will be told to be patient. We often waited 30 days to find out nothing was happening or it was incomplete in some way. We then had to fix the problem or sometimes start all over, wait another 30 days, and then fix those problems that cropped up. If you hope to be up and running in one month, lower your expectations. It may take four or five months, or longer, in reality. And, of course, you can't see anyone with insurance and bill it because it will be denied.

Payments will only start once you have a signed contract and are approved for electronic billing and/or electronic remittance advice (ERA). Most insurance companies want to pay electronically (EFT or electronic file transfer) which is usually good for the provider. Just watch for EOBs (explanation of benefits) that do not come directly to you because they had a zero-paid amount. I discovered you frequently have to hunt down the EOB instead of always expecting it to be sent to you. This can look on the surface like it was not processed or paid. Shoot for having all of them sent to you through your electronic billing company or some other method.

While we were getting set up with our electronic billing company, we also had to arrange for other subservices such as an insurance clearinghouse that processes the claims. In our case, we send the claim through our online medical billing software which sends it to the clearinghouse who then sends it to the insurance company. This allows for the information to be sent securely and in a form the insurance company can accept for processing. Our software uses Apex. We also had to set up a service to receive electronic remittance advice through our billing software. These two services added complexity and time.

Have someone else double-check your work when filling out insurance applications. I made one small mistake that caused months of delays. The questions on the applications are often ambiguous and it is hard to get clarity if you call, chat, or send emails. By working together, we were able to figure out correct answers and discover small mistakes that are costly both in terms of time and money. It is nearly impossible to correct the mistake once the paperwork has been sent.

A final problem was we did not realize many insurance companies required a completely new contract when we changed business operations. Many customer representatives do not seem to be trained to think about each individual's circumstances. Be sure to ask plenty of questions and don't assume the advice is correct. We closed one counseling business, retired that tax ID number, and opened a new business with a new tax ID. We were mistakenly told or at least led to believe the crossover would be simple since we were already credentialed with all the companies. We soon found this to not be true. We were required to start all over like we were new to the business and had never been credentialed. I was not surprised by that; I had just hoped it was not a requirement.

Start-up Tips:

- The sooner you start getting on insurance panels the better. You will need a tax ID, location address, email, business phone number, and possibly a fax line before you can initiate becoming a provider.

- If told to wait until you hear from the provider (typically a 3-6 month wait), do not just patiently wait. Of course, you will have to provide them with enough reasonable time to work on your case but, more often than not, we found there were problems the insurance companies did not actively tell us about. We would call to check on the status, be told it would take up to six months, and then find out later that our application was incomplete, or they did not receive something we had sent. Rarely did an insurance company notify us there was a problem without us calling to inquire.

One method I used is decidedly old-school but effective. I made two file folders for each insurance company. One was for work-in-progress notes and the other was for final letters of acceptance and contracts. You may prefer digital solutions but I find it quicker and easier to scan and find information when it is in paper format.

As I contacted each insurance company, I kept a running list of dates, times, and results of each contact I made. It was nearly impossible for me to keep all this information in my head. I could quickly glance and find out several weeks had passed and I needed to follow up with them. Whenever I had some time, I would pull out the folders and see what needed to be addressed. It was also nice to see the progress when I could put the folder to the side because it was complete. The folders also allowed me to keep detailed records of what I thought had happened.

Many times, I looked back at a note that said it was all resolved, only to discover later there was still an issue. I often questioned my sanity or at the very least my memory. Neither was off. I had to resend the same document multiple times to several companies who stated they never received it.

I combined my paper files with the Kanbanflow website mentioned earlier to track my to-do list for insurance companies. I especially liked how I could collaborate with my colleague on what she was working on so we didn't overlap in our efforts.

Start-up Tips:

- Keep documentation of everything. It is easy to get details confused and it is overwhelming with so many things happening at once. Keep emails, phone texts, documents, or other pertinent information.

- Do not assume things are working as planned, even if you have been told they are. It seems that companies are segmented enough that if a correction is made in one place, it does not necessarily mean it is communicated to all departments that need to know.

Importance of a Paper Trail

My colleague started a habit that became very important and useful. Because we were contacting many insurance providers, and other support companies, at one time, we created digital folders in our email to keep track of progress on an issue. After reading and taking action on an email, we would move it over to its appropriate folder for future reference if needed. It was nearly impossible to remember all the details and this provided us a way to keep up with it. Not only that, we could keep up with important contacts and email accounts that were responsive to our needs.

By the way, if you discover a contact who seems to be especially responsive and knowledgeable, by all means, keep their information. This occurred over and over again. There was almost always one individual who made the magic happen at their office and helped us with an issue. Many times, you may have to ask to have the problem elevated to a manager to correct something that is not usual business.

Location Selection

Our physical office space ended up being in an office building that was built in 1959 and had not been renovated since the 1970s. The initial walk-through showed paneled walls and brightly colored carpet. These things were easily updated. What we had not planned on, however, was that the electrical system, internet, plumbing, and telephone systems were also antiquated.

Older buildings can have a nice aesthetic that we particularly like. The view of downtown from the third floor was a major selling point. Two-thirds of each wall was glass, giving the offices beautiful, natural daylight. We felt the walls were sufficiently thick to provide sound insulation as we counseled our clients.

As we got deeper into the project, we discovered multiple problems. The walls were plaster, making them hard to work with and difficult to hang pictures. The landlord was responsible for providing the space but we were responsible for updating the interior. We clashed with the landlord over this. We felt the landlord should provide the basics of the shell and that we would only be responsible for painting and decorating.

The internet installation was all on us. The landlord stated each tenant would be responsible so they could choose internet providers. We felt the landlord should provide the basic cabling so we could choose which provider to hook up to. In the end, we compromised by purchasing some cable to extend the internet from the hallway to our office. The removal of old materials and paint was supplied by the landlord but we did purchase some interior paint to personalize our space.

One of the main problems with updating our space was the landlord hired an individual from out of state who claimed to be an electrician. His work was not only substandard but potentially dangerous. She had entrusted him to do work on the walls and lay carpet in addition to the electrical work. He took over two months to partially complete this project. Each week, for weeks, he would promise to finish in "two more days." This mantra became a source of frustration and a running joke for our staff. Ultimately, the landlord had to have someone come back in and spend a week correcting his dangerous electrical mistakes. Thankfully, we were not financially responsible for that.

As of this writing, we are in our new office space for a little over one year. We have settled in and we enjoy the new office, despite ongoing issues. The door to my office did not completely close, but I finally got that fixed. There are still small holes in the walls around several outlets, but they no longer hang perilously from the wall. The entire building is under renovation and should look very nice eventually.

It probably would have been much easier to choose a more up-to-date and move-in-ready space, but we saw the potential of a renovated downtown space and made that choice. Our second location choice was also downtown. It is now on a road that is under major construction for the next two years. This likely would have caused other problems for us had we chosen it. In the end, no space is perfect. Look at the pros and cons and make your best decision.

Another issue when choosing a location is to determine your needs and budget. How much space do you need for each therapist, a waiting area, and any other areas for files and storage? Once you have an idea of the square footage and start looking for spaces, you will see commercial office space listed in dollars per square foot per year. If you leased a 750-square-foot space at $14 per square foot per year, you would be looking at a monthly rent of around $875. To easily calculate this, divide 14 by 12 months and multiply by the square footage. Rent varies greatly around the country and you might have to look around to find something affordable. You want to have a nice, professional space but don't overspend and cause a financial burden.

Start-up Tips:

- Think ahead about what kind of problems may present if you lease a particular space. Ours did not have updated access to the internet, meaning there were no ethernet outlets. We overcame that by going with wireless internet versus trying to go through concrete and plaster walls to string cable. Our ceilings are also solid instead of a drop-ceiling where wires can be routed above the tiles.

- Try to temper your excitement about opening a business and take time to think about your choices. Ask plenty of questions and ask each other their opinions.

- Search yourself and your business online to ensure the information is correct and how you want it presented. Look at your information on more than one access point; in other words, check both mobile phone and media sites, different directories and search engines, Apple and Android, etc.

Contractor Issues

Nothing is more frustrating than having something outside of your control. This is one of those situations where counselors may have to apply the skills they teach others to themselves. The landlord, faced with difficulties in finding competent workers, hired someone who proclaimed to be a licensed electrician in another state. She failed to check his credentials.

This individual was not knowledgeable in electricity as he made numerous potentially dangerous mistakes in wiring the office we had leased. He also claimed he could hang drywall, paint, lay carpet, and do other jobs. This individual knew very little about any of these things. He attempted to put several layers of mud on the wall instead of hanging drywall over the old concrete wall that was covered with paneling. He painted multiple coats of the wrong color of paint. He left large holes in the walls around the outlets. He failed to cut the carpet along the edges of the wall, placing it under the baseboards which then failed to stick to the wall. When the plastic border did not adhere, he nailed it to the wall. Many electrical outlets did not work or had mud over the holes. Worst of all, we had very little leverage to make it right because the landlord had hired him and we had to pay rent without being able to move into the space for two months.

If you have ever had any renovations or construction work done on your home, you are aware that there are always delays in obtaining materials, getting the wrong materials delivered and then waiting for the right replacements, or running into problems that could not have been foreseen. Always expect the job to take much longer and cost more than expected. Even though I was aware of this, it was still very frustrating. After much pressure on the contractor, we were able to move in. The landlord thankfully hired new people and repaired the mistakes made by the first worker. Two electricians still needed a whole week to fix the mistakes in an 1100-square-foot office.

Start-up Tip:

• Choose contractors carefully. Ask others for referrals for contractors with whom they have had a good experience. Do not pay upfront for services.

Try to get detailed estimates in writing if you can. Do not pay until all the work is up to your standard, no matter how hard the contractor protests. Paid contractors are unmotivated to return to finish their job.

Premature Lease Agreement

We signed a lease for our office space at the end of July with the expectation we would move in by the end of August. Initially, we had planned to have the carpet removed and replaced, the walls painted, and a ten-foot-wide interior wall installed to divide a room and make another office. The interior wall only took a few days. Everything else took much longer even though they were relatively simple things to change.

Whatever your time frame is, expect delays, especially if any kind of construction or renovation has to occur. This is even more true if you have to hire others and depend on them showing up to do the work. If you have been involved in any kind of renovation work, you know to expect delays and unforeseen issues.

The delays on our project became an issue because we had signed the lease to start paying in August. We were caught between paying for the old location we were closing and paying for the new location we couldn't use. Thankfully, there was only one month of overlap but it could have been a major problem if it had gone on.

As for the lease agreement itself, we were offered 1, 3, and 5-year lease options. We made a decision in the moment and chose 3 years but, looking back now, time passes very quickly. I can't imagine we would pick up and relocate after three years. It has taken over a year just to get established. All of the headaches that would come with moving (i.e., change of address for all insurance companies and others with whom we do business), would not be desirable if we can avoid it.

Our landlord had to install a new roof on our office building and has spent significant money renovating the space. I imagine this will be reflected in our new lease when the time comes. Give serious consideration to your lease term when signing. Businesses that sell products can raise prices to cover overhead but for a service business like counseling, it is harder. This is especially true if the majority of your clients have insurance. Insurance contracts rarely raise payments to providers and you are not allowed to bill the client for more than your contracted rate.

Start-up Tips:

- Try to find a space that needs little, if any, renovation. If it does, try to ensure the renovations are complete before signing a lease or you have the skills to do the renovations yourself.

- Think about the length of the lease you want to sign. We chose 3 years but now, with rents rising rapidly across the country, we wonder if we should have chosen a longer lease. We were offered 1, 3, and 5. We don't plan on moving after all it took to establish our office. Consider your long-term plans when choosing a length for your lease.

Communications

It seems that texting has replaced telephone calls and email as the communication method of choice. Leaving phone messages often results in someone never listening to the message and then calling back to see why you called. Emails often go unread for days or longer. Text is easy, accessible, and usually read within a short period.

One downfall of this method, however, is the possibility of miscommunication. The tone of voice, body language, volume, and other important information must be inferred. Often incorrectly. We discovered there had been some miscommunication between the landlord and us regarding the landlord's contractor. This easily could have resulted in conflict had we not met in person and corrected our assumptions.

Start-up Tips:

- Texting is fine for minor communication but, if something could be misunderstood, opt for a phone call instead. You might also want to consider an email so you have a written document to refer back to if there is a misunderstanding. You might want to save important emails in a folder on your computer or phone so you can refer to them if needed.

- Find out the preferred method of contacting the person with whom you are engaging for work. You are more likely to get a quick response if you use their preferred method.

- Be sure both parties are clear on expectations.

Location details

You may be so excited about opening your private practice that you get overwhelmed or overlook small details. On the other hand, you may be very observant and detail-oriented. Either way, pay close attention to details about your new space that may matter later. If you have ever purchased or rented property, you are likely more aware of the importance of doing this.

For example, think about the layout of your office and the location of outlets, windows, concrete walls, etc. It is easier to correct this before moving in. In my case, several outlets were added but were installed incorrectly, causing a potential fire hazard. Several new outlets did not even work. Many outlets were near each other, limiting the flexibility of where to locate items. I have one long wall with no outlets. Two vents in the ceiling of two offices provide no airflow. The building is old and required new telephone and networking wiring even though some was present.

The process of choosing a location is much like buying a used car. Check out all the details for potential problems and address them before signing the lease or moving in. Don't just assume it works. I found it harder to get the landlord to address things of this nature once we had moved in, despite having a good landlord.

We also chose office space with large windows. This has been both a blessing and a curse. Large windows provide beautiful sunlight that lifts the mood of both the counselor and the client. We also have great views from the third floor. The downside is they can be drafty in winter and hot in summer.

Soundproofing is important to any counselor. We understand the need for confidentiality and have always used sound machines to create gray noise. In our new location, however, the acoustics surprised us. We might not be able to hear one another on each side of the waiting area but someone at the other end of the hallway outside of our suite would be able to hear conversations like they were in the same room. We had to get creative to ensure confidentiality. We carefully placed several sound machines, used soft surfaces, and arranged furniture to meet our needs. Even if you occupy the entire building, you want to ensure there is a sound barrier between the counselor's offices and the treatment and public areas.

We also found that clients' impressions made a difference in our choice of office space. Our old office space was located in a home, making it easy to separate clients so confidentiality was not an issue. They liked the space but hated the parking situation. The parking allowed for up to six cars at a time but required everyone to turn around and parallel park.

The new location has a large parking lot but now clients are reluctant to use the fifty-year-old elevator to get to our suite. They were also turned off by the look of unfinished space in the building that was waiting for a tenant before being refurbished. That problem has eventually taken care of itself as office space has been leased out but it did look abandoned early on. Homeless people in our downtown make a negative impression as people enter our building.

When preparing your office space, think about the order in which things need to be done. We had contacted someone to install our computer network before realizing the old networking wiring was not usable. We then had to rewire our space and found out that networking the computers would be done more efficiently by Wi-Fi than by hardwiring them. In the end, we didn't need the computer networking consultant or the computer cable after all.

If you don't feel confident about these types of things, you may want to ask a friend or someone with experience to help you look for potential problems as you prepare to move into your new space.

Start-up Tip:

• The location of your business is an important decision. Ensure you have enough space for adding a future therapist if you desire to expand. Minor inconveniences that interfere with everyday duties can grow into major annoyances. Some things are harder to correct once you have moved in.

3 SETTING UP FOR BUSINESS

Problems Finding Information

Because businesses are started every day, you would imagine there would be all kinds of information available to assist you in the process. I found very little information to guide us through the process, hence, this book. Most information online is very general and typically includes only a few paragraphs. All the entities with whom you will have to engage to get your business started are working independently. Hence, there is no clear flow of what steps to take, whom to contact, and when. Banks, liability insurance companies, behavioral health insurance companies, state websites, etc. are not forthcoming with the steps that connect you to them or follow-up contacts once they have done their portion. They all are acting independently of one another.

My frustration over trying to find clear answers to a common process motivated me to write this book. People open businesses daily yet there was not much online to guide me. Any information I did find was not coordinated or connected to other aspects of opening a business.

Another thing became apparent in our journey. We soon discovered that we had to be detectives, using our deductive reasoning skills to uncover sources of problems. Sometimes the tiniest incorrect thing can cause multitudes of problems.

I made a mistake on one insurance application, checking a box that I might want to do online insurance billing through their website. In my mind, I was giving myself an opportunity for flexibility while I was waiting for billing through our clearinghouse to be set up. This one mistake ended up causing at least a six-month delay in setting up this insurance company, which incidentally was our largest. I would call and ask about the status of my application and would be told everything was in order, and we even received an acceptance letter. I was told to wait on billing until I had received an e-commerce letter. I finally received that letter one year later.

The only way the problem got resolved was I found the name, email address, and phone number of a manager willing to take the time to help me figure out what was wrong with my application. That mistake was the reason I couldn't get that insurance company set up with the third-party billing clearinghouse. I attempted to bill during the interim since I got the acceptance letter and a contract, but nearly all sessions were denied.

Insurance companies (the ones we had to get credentialed with to see our clients) did not tell us we needed a new contract with them. If you recall, we had already been in private practice and were closing one business to open another. They initially said only a letter and W-9 were sufficient but we discovered months later it was not. Nearly all companies wanted a new contract. Our situation was somewhat different than someone new to the field. We had been contracted with multiple insurance companies for years. In the end, we needed new contracts because we had a new tax ID. We had hoped it would make credentialing quicker and easier to have already been credentialed but it didn't.

Start-up Tips:

- It will take much longer than expected for things to take place.
- No one told us we needed to file certain paperwork with the state offices.
- A change of address was needed with the IRS once we moved. It caused a problem with Medicare not approving a contract because of the mismatch in addresses. We remembered to update changes with most things but this easily slipped our minds. Be sure to inform everyone of your change of address, not just depending on the post office change of address form.

One thing depends on another

Something not initially in our awareness was how many things depended on something else before they could be done. For instance, we could not open a bank account without a leased office space. We could not open a business credit card until we had been in business for over a year or supplied more personal information and proof than was required when I purchased a home. We could not do anything without a business name and address. A post office box was often not acceptable. Obtaining a lease meant we would be responsible for rent before we could produce income. Many insurance companies would not allow electronic funds transfers until we had a cashed check from them. We could not get a check from them because we were waiting months to get credentialed. We couldn't get a business phone number without a business address. We didn't want to pay for a business telephone until we had a location to use it.

Start-up Tip:

- Use my start-up checklist to ensure you are working on items in the most efficient way.

Financial matters

At this point, you have probably not earned any income, but plan for how you will pay yourself or do payroll if you choose an LLC or S Corp.

We spent several months trying to determine how much to pay ourselves as an S Corp.

It is a more complicated pay structure than other business types. The advantage of this type is you can take a relatively smaller salary (that is taxable) and get the remainder of your pay as a distribution, which is non-taxable.

I searched many books and websites trying to determine how much should come from salary versus distribution. We were told by the first accountant to take about half in salary. I'm not sure she interviewed us enough to know our particular situation. She stated it was how she ran her business and she strongly recommended it for us. A colleague of mine stated he believed an S Corp was only beneficial if you earn over $80,000 a year and I tend to agree.

What you don't want to do is receive too much from distributions because this alerts the IRS that you may be avoiding paying taxes, resulting in penalties and destroying the benefit of being an S Corp. We accidentally took too much from our distribution account and had to pay a small fee as a result. This happened after we took nothing for three months and then all of our pay for the fourth month from distribution. We thought keeping it at about 25% would be acceptable but, it wasn't.

Most websites and books, as well as the IRS, tell you to take a "reasonable" salary, an amount that is reasonable for your occupation. We found that no one, even accountants, has an exact amount to tell you or even a way to calculate it for yourself.

Because salaries vary quite a bit, depending on where you live and work, I utilized the website www.onetonline.org to determine this amount. Under "occupation keyword search," type in your specific occupation and you will be presented with a whole list of similar occupations. Choose the one that matches you best, scroll down to almost the bottom of the page and you will find an area where you can find the median wage for the country, your state, city, and even down to the zip code. I used the median figure for my zip code. This will provide you with an expected salary if you are new to the field or just want to know where you stand in comparison to others. By the way, I often use this resource with clients who are exploring careers.

As it turned out, I didn't need this figure after all. We decided it was best for our business to just get paid what each of us earned individually, minus expenses and some left over. We were making it unnecessarily complicated.

We determined our pay using this formula:

Gross income - expenses - cushion left in bank account = take-home pay.

Let's make up some numbers to see how the formula would work. If I brought in $ 5,000 gross income in one month, took out $1,000 in expenses and taxes, and left $500 as a cushion, my take-home pay would be $3,500. Once there is a reasonable cushion for a varying income and unexpected expenses, you can cut back or eliminate the cushion. I tend to follow the personal financial advice to keep at least three to six months of income in an account for hard times and apply this to business financials as well. The lower your expenses, the better off you will be.

This was the formula we ended up with. We were spending way too much time fretting over how much to leave in the "distribution" pile and inadvertently took too much out of distribution initially. This can completely mess up the whole concept of an S Corp so be careful.

We finally settled on paying ourselves a working salary with a varying dollar amount left over each month to cover unexpected expenses/distribution. Our tax advisor let us know we could take "distributions" out as a year-end bonus or to help cover health care expenses. We were too focused on trying to figure it out each month since we were new to the concept and didn't want to create a problem down the road. This took a lot of stress off me because I was leaving too much behind each month and stressing over my personal finances in the first few months. Just think of distributions as profit from your work, above your usual salary. Distributions can be in many forms, such as payment for benefits like insurance or as a bonus. Distributions are pre-tax money so it helps save on your personal taxes in the long run.

The formula gets a little more complicated when you include additional employees/owners. Because of our confusion over the terms of an S Corp and incorrectly believing everything had to be 50/50 when it came to getting a salary, we stumbled in this area. We eventually figured out that salaries can be completely different, it is the distribution that has to follow percentages of ownership. The percentages are based on your initial articles of incorporation and how you set things up. Most people might choose a 50/50 ownership agreement but it can be any combination. You might choose 51/49 so one person has more control and the final decision-making power. It could also benefit you to have a minority as a 51 percent owner to enable eligibility for grants and loans to women and minorities.

We decided for our two-person business to track how much gross income each person generated, share the expenses equally, and then leave the remainder for unexpected expenses and distribution at a later point. Distributions are the profit left over from your work. It might be tempting to take home more income but remember the whole point of an S Corp is the remainder is tax-free income you will still receive in some form.

We felt it would have been unfair to divide the income equally. This is especially true if someone is out for a significant period or goes to part-time work. In the end, it comes down to how the business is set up when created and explained in the details of the agreement or articles of incorporation. I strongly recommend taking the time to create these documents to prevent misunderstandings or worse later on. We were unsure how to handle this issue for a long time. Our incomes will never be the same each month so this is our solution. For the longest time, we thought the pay had to be the same for each of us.

As for the 51/49 split, or whatever you decide for your business if choosing an S Corp, it doesn't come into play until someone decides to buy or sell their portion of the business. This could be due to multiple reasons, including but not limited to, retirement, illness, or wanting less responsibility.

Start-up Tip:

- If you choose an S Corp as the structure of your business, take time to make sure you understand how it works. Overpaying yourself from the distribution account will result in fees that negate the benefits of creating the S Corp to begin with.

Income Delays

When our friend who decided to retire early announced her plans, the remaining partner and I immediately began planning how we would run the business. We had hoped that transitioning from one business to another business (different tax ID but the same providers minus one) would be a relatively smooth transition. We discovered it was for a couple of insurance providers but not for most. Expect it to take about six months on average for insurance companies to provide you with a contract but a few took up to a year. They may or may not offer back pay for clients seen before the contract is signed.

You could see clients as self-pay in the meantime but this might limit you. On the other hand, you might decide that self-pay is the way to go and not be tied to the insurance side of things. Many clinicians are now choosing 100% self-pay and not taking insurance at all. I see this trend continuing as people become more and more dissatisfied with the corporate greed and hand-tying insurance companies engage in.

If you are a social worker, you most likely accept Medicare or are interested in accepting it. Medicare is often one of the most frustrating to work with and takes the longest. After about 10 months, we were finally able to get Medicare payments processed correctly. This was after many hours of phone calls, updating the information online, repeatedly sending documents, and pleading for help. It was so stressful we had spontaneous shouts of joy when the first payments started coming though. Be sure you have enough savings and/or operating income to cover expenses while you are getting credentialed with insurance providers.

A recent development in this industry is the allowance of mental health counselors to start becoming Medicare providers. This will apply to those licensed as counselors and marriage and family therapists. They will be able to accept Medicare starting January 1, 2024. If you fall in this category and want more information on enrollment as a provider, I highly recommend Barbara Griswold's website, www.theinsurancemaze.com as a source of information. Accepting Medicare is a complex process so I defer you to more knowledgeable professionals.

As for Medicare websites, you will want to bookmark this cms.gov site, which is the portal for enrollment. This will guide you through the steps to take to become a provider. You are expected to opt out if you do not want to become a provider.

Start-up Tips:

- Just as financial advisors tell us to have 3-6 months of income in a rainy-day fund, you will need at least this amount to get you through the first few months while you are waiting to get on insurance panels. This would apply to both your personal and business finances. You can, of course, see clients on a self-pay basis while you are waiting. This brought in enough income for us to keep afloat but our take-home pay after expenses was low for the first six months. Don't count on being paid from insurance for a while.

- Make sure you understand how you intend to pay yourself and others and the methods you will use to make that happen.

Liability Insurance

You will need to acquire professional liability (malpractice) insurance. Some companies to consider are

HPSO, Lockton, and CPH. Goodtherapy.com states that you can expect to pay between $350 and $1,750 annually for $1,000,000/$3,000,000 coverage. We have been using CPH and are satisfied. If you belong to a professional organization, check them for discounted insurance plans.

If you rent a space, you would be advised to consider a general business liability policy in case of client accidents or being unable to work due to damage to the building, for example. Your landlord's policies will not cover your business per se. We found State Farm to be affordable at $33 a month or $396 annually.

Hiring employees or contractors

When we closed the old counseling business, we decided to continue the services of our secretary. You might want to look at your budget and determine if you can afford a secretary at least part-time. The only con I can think of is you have someone you will have to pay each month. The benefits of having a secretary are numerous.

Our secretary works two and a half days each week. We have her do all the tasks that don't bring in revenue. This frees the counselors up to see clients and complete paperwork. In our office, the counselors also do the billing as we are more aware of the specifics of each client. Utilizing online electronic health records makes billing fast and easy.

Our secretary answers the phone, deals with questions from potential and current clients, helps make appointments and take payments, takes care of all paperwork and mailing, balances the checkbook, and pays bills. She gathers the demographic information and checks the potential clients' insurance deductibles, copay, and other pertinent information when new clients call. When payments come in, she alerts us, and then we post them to our EHR.

We could have her do this step but that is how we do it in our office. If you set up electronic remittance advice and electronic file transfer through your EHR, posting payments is quick and easy.

The secretary also prepares information for the tax preparer at the end of the year. One very helpful benefit of having a secretary is she can spend the countless hours on hold that is sometimes required when calling insurance companies or other vendors. Having to schedule large blocks of time out of our counseling appointments to handle these issues is not a very efficient use of our time.

Electronic billing companies

Choosing an EHR can be a daunting task. There are dozens of options to choose from. Many of those available are suited more for very large hospitals and corporations. I am focusing on just a select few to not overwhelm you with choices. Ultimately, the EHR that is right for you will depend on your particular circumstances. I will review some things to consider when choosing a vendor and hope it will make your decision easier.

One thing I encountered when searching for an EHR was that most of the comparison websites looked suspiciously like hidden ads that would direct you to their product. They accomplished this by downplaying the attributes of the competitors and upselling the positive attributes of their own. There is nothing wrong with advertising, of course, just pay attention to what you are reading.

Most of them offer a free trial. I recommend picking a couple you are seriously considering and taking advantage of the free trial so you can compare them with sample data.

In our search for a vendor, we had already been in private practice under a partnership. This heavily influenced our decision in choosing which provider. Several years ago, the partners had chosen MyClientsPlus and their EHR. At that time, electronic health records were just becoming available and the partners used MyClientsPlus just for billing and posting payments. We decided to stay with MyClientsPlus for several reasons. We were familiar with the software and could easily transfer current clients to the new business. The prices are reasonable. Those were the main selling points. It was recently acquired by TherapyBrands, a company that is actively working to update and make its software user-friendly. Several EHR companies have very outdated software and I would not consider using them.

One thing you might want to consider is going for the annual subscription plan versus the monthly. MyClientsPlus has a 15% savings for annual subscriptions. This will save us over $100 a year in our office. When you think about it, it is a no-brainer because you most likely will not change providers once you have one. You could always sign on as monthly in the beginning and once you are more financially stable, change over to annual status. This also gives you adequate time to try out the service.

As the field has evolved, most if not all vendors offer a full suite of services which you should consider when setting up your practice.

Some of the services offered include

1. Electronic billing
2. Electronic scheduling by the office staff
3. Patient portal for online scheduling and bill payment by the client
4. Creation of client statements
5. ERA (electronic remittance advice) and EFT (electronic funds transfer)
6. Ability to see the whole group's schedule at once

7. Email, text, and phone appointment reminders

8. Telehealth integration

9. Credit card acceptance and processing

A good comparison website for EHR I discovered is Selecthub. I had selected a company size of 2-5 employees to narrow down the selection. You can set the filters to your specifications similar to purchasing an item from an online retailer.

Some contenders with excellent reviews on selecthub.com include:

1. TherapyBrands - includes MyClientsPlus, TheraNest

2. SimplePractice

3. TherapyNotes

4. ICANotes

5. Jane app

Take your time in making a selection because it can be difficult and time-consuming to start over on another platform. Be sure to read the fine print because SimplePractice has made the news recently regarding terms and conditions that may provide them with noncancellable access to your information. Think about how you prefer or would prefer to do your notes and billing before choosing.

While the industry has been going towards a digital solution for paperwork, there are both positives and negatives to this approach. Digital solutions allow you to type notes so they are legible and anyone can read them, access them from any place via the internet, store them in a location offsite in case of fire or other disaster, and are just basically convenient. Some of the negatives would be lack of access in case of an internet outage and the potential for the company to go out of business but they should provide access even then. I also like having the ability to shuffle through multiple pages to find something and that seems easier for me with a physical file.

The positives of a physical file on each client are easy access to information, easier for the less technically savvy, and you aren't looking at a computer while talking with your client. The downsides include the need for physical storage that is HIPAA-compliant, the possibility of being damaged by fire, water, or other disaster, and the inconvenience of having to copy a record to send it electronically or by mail.

As for the paperwork itself, if you work or worked for a counseling office, you probably did not have to create your paperwork. A digital EHR usually has multiple examples of necessary documents you may use on their platform. You get to choose which ones match your needs best.

If you have to create paperwork yourself, there are options on websites where you can download a whole folder of necessary electronic documents. You can either use them electronically or print them out for your use. Check out etsy.com, privatepracticestartup.com, practiceofthepractice.com, and theinsurancemaze.com. I have not personally vetted the forms on these websites, but I believe them to be excellent sources.

You would want to have these forms ready to go before seeing clients. Make multiple paper copies with a saved master copy or a saved digital master so you don't accidentally overwrite your files. If using digital files, open up a fresh one each time because it is easy to get into the habit of overwriting a previous document and increasing the chance of typographical errors.

HIPAA compliance

If you have worked at all in the mental health field, you are aware of HIPAA, which stands for the Health Insurance Portability and

Accountability Act. The scope of this book is not to educate you on this topic, which is extensive, but to ensure you comply and know where to locate the information.

Go to the HealthIT.gov website and download the HIPAA risk assessment tool. This will guide you on what your business needs to be compliant. Its focus is on the protection of electronic health information. It also addresses client access to medical records. When you create your business and client documentation, you will want to ensure it meets these requirements.

I also highly recommend personcenteredtech.com. Their focus is on these types of topics that counselors generally feel a lack of knowledge and understanding.

There are several forms you will want to consider creating or purchasing for your new office. You may choose paper or digital formats or a combination of the two. I had originally hoped to digitize our documents and have clients sign digitally but that is a future project. I plan to use something like an iPad and software that collects a digital signature.

Here are some suggestions for forms you will need:

1.   Demographics sheet - Includes items such as basic client contact information, insurance, referral source, and the reason for seeking therapy.

2.   Releases of information - You will want to obtain releases for healthcare providers (most insurance contracts require this), insurance providers, and previous treatment providers if applicable.

3.   Insurance form - We include details about deductibles, copays, and coinsurance. We have the client sign this form so they know their charges.

4.   Good faith estimate - A new law requires you to inform self-pay clients of an estimate of what they will be charged and how many visits they can expect to have. This is signed by the client.

5.   HIPAA notice/Informed consent - This form informs clients of their privacy rights and access to medical information. We obtain a signature on this. We have the longer explanation available but no one generally wants that as they are familiar with this from visiting healthcare providers.

6.   Policies - Inform the client of your policies about extra charges, fees for no-shows, cancellation policy, after-hours calls, emergency procedures, and other pertinent information. This, too, is signed.

7.   Confidentiality - You want to educate your client about confidentiality and whether or not they will allow you to send mail or leave phone messages.

You will also need forms for conducting business. These forms would include:

1.   Biopsychosocial intake - You want a separate intake for adults and children. If you work with couples, you probably might want a third one specifically designed for that purpose.

2.   Treatment plan - This form should contain clear, specific goals and a list of specific interventions for achieving those goals. You will want to include a time frame, an indication of when they are achieved, and update the goals regularly. Most therapists seem to have trouble following through with treatment plans.   Some online mental health billing platforms include treatment planning as an option. While you may have to pay extra for this feature, it can be time-saving and take some off your workload.

3.   Progress notes - Progress notes should include the client and counselor's names, date of service, type of service (CPT code), length, beginning and ending times, who was present in the session, and whether it was in person or via telehealth. The body of the note should include the client's problem being addressed, a note about safety (suicidal/homicidal, etc.), your specific intervention to address the problem, the next date of

service, and your signature. I have recently started using the progress note template offered by Barbara Griswold after I attended one of her seminars. Her website is www.theinsurancemaze.com.

4. Progress measures - This one is not essential; however, including a method of measuring your client's initial symptoms and then measuring progress is advisable. This can not only inform you and your client whether or not they are making progress, but it can also show insurance companies measurable results. You can accomplish this in several different ways. There are some progress measurement tools available, such as PCOMS, or you could do a pre-and post-test of various questionnaires.

At my office, I settled on a hybrid solution of digital and paper forms, which works best for me. I use a digital EHR for billing and tracking payments. I use a digital copy of a treatment plan and progress note that I print out and put in my physical folder after filling it out on my laptop. We also use a backup system of index cards with critical client information on them. Surprisingly, these are often needed. That way we can contact clients when the internet or a particular website is down. You could also use your EHR to print out a physical report of this information occasionally but we don't do that. There have been times when the internet or electricity was down but we were still able to operate because of these physical documents and backups.

Those forms address the client services side of your business. You also want to create a manual of policies and procedures for the operations side. This doesn't have to be especially formal. Having clear-cut policies will help in day-to-day operations and assist you by planning ahead of time. Some suggested items to include are:

Policies (your rules):

1. No show, missed appointment, cancellation policy, and fees if any

2. Late arrival policy

3. Session charges and types of payment

4. Charges for extra services such as filling out disability forms, drafting letters that clients request, medical records requests

5. HIPAA compliance and security

6. Inclement Weather

7. Client communication (email, phone, social media, etc.)

8. Crisis management of clients

9. Disaster and crisis management of the business

10. Telehealth

11. Controlled substances and weapons

12. Confidentiality

Procedures (how you conduct business):

1. Storage of client files

2. Business agreements with vendors and contractors

3. Billing clients and vendors/expectation of payment

4. HIPAA compliance and documentation of how your office has addressed it

5. Security

6. New client intake procedure

Start-Up tips:

•   Take time to try out demos of electronic health record/billing websites and programs. This is something you will use daily and is difficult to change once you have committed.

Policy and Procedure Manuals

Writing policy and procedure manuals is not a fun task for most people. It does not have to be as formal as ones you may have come across in large organizations but it is beneficial to have some general guidelines. For example, you can avoid the embarrassment of looking unprepared when someone asks you how much you charge to fill out disability paperwork or even whether you do that sort of thing (yes, this has happened to me). Also, if there is more than one provider, you will be consistent in your answers.

1. Welcome Letter
2. HIPAA
3. Consent, Policies & Agreement
4. Release of Information
5. Process/Progress Notes
6. Good Faith Estimate
7. Biopsychosocial (3 different forms for minors, adults & couples)
8. Good Faith Estimate
9. Treatment Plan
10. Documentation/Communication Form
11. Suicide Risk Assessment
12. Substance Abuse Intake

Client management is one area to consider. What is your no-show policy? What are your fees for filling out forms, writing letters, and sending copies of documents? What are your hours of business? How does someone access emergency services? How do you handle vacation and sickness coverage? How do you handle delinquent accounts when clients have not paid their bills?

Employee/contractor management is another area. Your manual developed from creating an LLC or S Corp should address many of these issues. Do you plan on doing annual evaluations? What if you hire independent contractors? How would you discipline employees or consider raises? What is the hiring process if you need part-time help?

Business management might include things like business agreements with independent contractors and others who may come into your office to do work. What is your policy on enforcing HIPAA? Who is responsible for various aspects of the business?

Document Management

Something I have particularly found useful is the ability to store files in the cloud so I can access them from anywhere. Of course, I am careful not to store things with clients' personal information but I do save copies of files and forms I have created. Sometimes I work on them from somewhere other than the office. Having the digital copy available is helpful when sharing files with others. It also is a lifesaver if your computer malfunctions. We all know we should be backing up our files but few of us do it consistently. You do not, of course, want to save unencrypted files with sensitive client data to these sites, as that would be a violation of HIPAA rules.

Logo creation

We wanted to create a professional appearance but were limited in financial resources. After trying out multiple websites, I settled on www.logo.com as the best place to create a new logo for our company. It was easy to use, much of it is free and you can download usable logos in various sizes and configurations. I used these logos to create our professional stationery, applied it to all our forms, made business cards, and even used it for the sign on our door.

A logo is not necessary for a business but can make it look more professional. It can also help people recognize your business, differentiating it from others. I waited until about one year into the new business before I settled on the final one because we focused our energy on more important matters.

It took a while to choose a logo but our business looks much more professional as a result. Our logo is present on all of our paperwork that others will see, online, and on our door sign.

Marketing

Marketing your practice will depend on multiple factors. In my case, we had an established caseload and we were moving to another location. The fact we were changing our name and tax ID was really of no importance to our clients.

We did have to take into consideration how we would continue to attract new clients, even though our caseloads are often full. We have depended on Psychology Today profiles and client word-of-mouth. Most of our referrals come from these sources. The next category is referrals from other providers, mainly healthcare providers.

Here are some other factors to consider in regards to marketing your practice:

- Location visibility and signage
- Networking with other providers in person and online

- Online presence - your company website if you have one, Google business website, LinkedIn, etc.

- Logo, business cards, pens, and possibly brochures. Your brand name and logo on items you provide to clients can help get the word out.

- Responsiveness to client phone calls and requests for information. It is amazing how often clients state they called numerous therapists for an appointment and no one called them back.

- Other methods to get the word out locally, such as attending health fairs, or speaking on the radio about a mental health topic.

Most of these ideas require little time or money. The demand for counseling is high and once the public knows about your office, getting clients should be fairly easy.

Nick Kolenda has an interesting (to me, at least) newsletter about the psychology of marketing. You can find some useful tips to make your marketing efforts as effective as possible. I also enjoy reading how marketing works from a psychological point of view.

Start-up tips:

- Look at lots of examples of forms other therapists use and combine them into the best for your needs. Or, take the easier route and purchase some that are already prepared for use. The downside is they may not be exactly what you need.

- The marketing needs of our business are small. Many newbie therapists and counselors can easily overestimate what they need to purchase (in regards to business cards, signage, ads, etc.), and how much they need to spend in this area.

Resources

The resources listed in this section are ones I find especially useful in my practice. You may have heard of most of them, depending on how long you have been working in the field.

Psychology Today and other referral sources

I have read reviews from other counselors who dislike Psychology Today as a source for referrals but it has been my experience that the majority of our referrals come from it. Years ago, we paid nearly $400 a year to be included in the local phone directory. As times have changed and phone directories are rarely utilized, most people now use the internet for searching. We stopped purchasing space in the phone directory and tried out other options. Psychology Today has consistently been a relatively inexpensive way to reach our target audience.

There are several benefits to using Psychology Today. The website is very easy to use and set up. Making updates is simple. You can post a photo of yourself and now video introductions are included. Use these tools to set yourself apart from the competition.

Speaking of competition, Psychology Today can be useful in checking on who your competitors are in your area. As a counselor or social worker, you probably are not used to thinking of colleagues as competitors but, from a business sense, they are. Find out what types of therapy they provide, what insurance providers they work with, and what their rates are. When doing a business comparison, which I highly recommend before starting your business, this site can be a good source of information. Find out the strengths and weaknesses of your competitors. Do a SWOT analysis (this stands for strengths, weaknesses, opportunities, and threats) as indicated at the beginning of the book.

Probably our second strongest source of referrals is from satisfied customers. I think this says a lot about the quality of our services. It is the highest compliment to have one of your clients say they want to refer friends and family to you for counseling.

CAQH

CAQH, the Council for Affordable Quality Healthcare, is a website that eliminates duplication of paperwork and allows insurance companies to interact with your information in one central place. Many insurance companies will require you to have a profile on this website so creating one will be one of the first things you do in the credentialing process.

New laws require therapists and social workers to update their business information every 90 days. CAQH is one place that assists with that requirement. By uploading your documents once to this site, insurance companies can find what they need and keep you credentialed.

Availity

Availity serves to streamline communication between healthcare stakeholders. I have not found it to be especially easy and intuitive to use. Not all insurance providers are represented but you can use it to find benefits, update the 90-day business information requirement, and look up payments. Looking up payments is becoming more of an issue as insurance companies stop sending postal correspondence with EOBs or checks.

Software options

There are many software options to help you run your business efficiently and as cost-effectively as possible.

In the past, many businesses relied on Microsoft Office for their business needs. This was costly, especially if you needed access on several computers. It became a little more affordable when they changed to a subscription service. I often relied on the free app versions of Word, Excel, and PowerPoint. I found them to be adequate for my needs, as they offer a pretty good complement of features. When I taught a college-level course, I was able to use the full Office suite for free. I'm not sure everyone is aware that Microsoft offers Office free for college students and teachers.

A recent development has made Office software even more accessible for the budget-conscious. I have used Google Chrome as my default browser for years but Microsoft Edge deserves consideration. In addition to useful features such as a calculator, translator, and other tools, Edge now offers the main components of Office, called Office 365, within the browser itself, for free. A new tool for therapists is the artificial intelligence tool available in most browsers. Edge has Bing Chat. This can assist you in writing letters and Edge offers improved grammar and spellchecking.

Before switching to Edge to use Office apps, I had tried several other options. My preferred solution for documents was Google Docs and I still frequently use it. I like how my documents are saved and accessible from any computer. I can look at something at home and then continue working on the same document at the office without doing anything to make it happen. This document was created on Google Docs. The primary reason for using Edge is the compatibility with the .doc extension.

Other programs I have tried and used to some degree include OpenOffice, LibreOffice, and WPS. These three programs feel very old school but familiar at the same time. They do have some compatibility issues and are not as easily accessible as Office 365 on Edge or Google Docs on any browser.

Another free option is Microsoft To Do. I was surprised at how useful it is. Some of the best features for me are how you can assign a date but also can choose not to, and how it can be attached to the taskbar at the bottom so it is an easy reminder to check my to-do list. I tried several other to-do lists and found them to be too complicated and not useful because of "features" like forcing me to give a task a due date. Sometimes the simplest option is the best.

You will want to ensure any website or software you purchase or use in your new business is HIPAA-compliant. Look for information about this and obtain a business agreement. The folks at Person-Centered Tech are always up-to-date on all things related to HIPAA.

Doxy.me is a useful phone app and website for doing HIPAA-compliant therapy. The free version has worked okay but if you want more functionality, a paid version is available. I often have connectivity problems with doxy.me so you might want to look at other options. I like its ease of use but other colleagues have reported spotty performance as well.

Psychology Today has an option called Sessions that is HIPAA-compliant and free for anyone with a profile. I like having a professional profile on this site but other professionals have complained about some of their practices. I consistently get quality referrals from people searching for a therapist and finding me on this website. When our practice gets full, we inform clients to look there for a therapist. I like how you can sort by distance, type of counseling, type of clients, etc.

Accounting

There are several options for accounting, QuickBooks (www.quickbooks.intuit.com) being the best-known choice. Other options include FreshBooks and Wave. I probably would have chosen Wave if I had been on my own but we already owned a copy of QuickBooks. It didn't make sense to switch.

The website https://www.pcmag.com/picks/the-best-small-business-accounting-software has a great review of several accounting packages.

QuickBooks has both online and desktop versions. We ran into difficulties many times because we own the desktop version and chose the online version of payroll. One would think they would be very compatible but we had to call several times to get them working together. I recommend you do the online version if you plan on using QuickBooks for payroll. As a side note, QuickBooks is quite expensive for doing payroll for a couple of employees. We have discovered there are other local options and some online options but we chose QuickBooks for better compatibility.

The best thing about Wave is you can use it for free. The worst thing about Wave is you have to pay if you need payroll support. PCMag gives it 4.5 out of 5 stars, equal to QuickBooks.

I also seriously considered FreshBooks. It is best for sole proprietors and small businesses. It scores 4.5 stars out of 5 as well and is only about $15.00 per month. QuickBooks is double that at $30.00 per month to start.

Online Assistance

Mentaya.com

I have not personally used this service, but I find it interesting and may check into it at some point. Therapists refer their clients to the service and they handle insurance claim submissions and any problems that arise.

Headway.com

Headway is similar to Mentaya in regards to processing insurance claims but also advertises a service for getting clinicians credentialed. Credentialing is a time-consuming headache and this might be a solution. I have not personally used this service and cannot vouch for them.

Heard.com

Heard is a more recent entrant into the field of accounting that is specifically designed for therapists. An accountant married a therapist and recognized the need for these services. They cover payroll, bookkeeping, and taxes, and address the needs of S Corps. I particularly like their newsletter and articles that clearly and simply explain these terms in ways therapists and other mental health professionals can understand.

Services of this nature seem to be appearing regularly so you might want to see if any of them appeal to you. You have to decide how much your time is worth and whether it would help to outsource this work. To some degree, you benefit by having hands-on experience and understanding at an intimate level of how all this works.

Start-up tip:

• Some resources provide services that meet the needs of a therapist entering business but they tend to focus on one small area. Use this book to create a collection of the sites you find most beneficial. My goal was to make that process easier for you.

4 OPEN FOR BUSINESS!

I updated our business information on Google but found out I had a personal business website I had never seen before. This had incorrect information and I did not know it even existed. Google yourself as a business (your name and the business name), not just your personal name. If you don't have a Google business website, type on the Google website "google my business" and it will take you to a place to register your business. I highly recommend ensuring you are listed, as most of our clients find us through a Google search. Google is good at providing you with statistics about your business. Check it often to find out how clients are finding you. For us, they search "counseling" and the name of our city. You might have used social worker or therapist on your website but the average individual looking for us uses the term "counseling." Other search terms were CBT, cognitive-behavioral therapy, and marriage counseling.

You might want to check other search engines and referral sites like healthgrades.com or findatherapist.com. They compile your information from different sources and it is often outdated. Either ask them to remove your information or correct mistakes.

Financial management

Key Performance Indicators (KPIs) are statistics you want to track for your business. There are many possibilities and some are not as applicable for a counseling office. Some of the basic KPIs could include gross income, gross profit, net profit, profit margin, cost per session, average revenue per session, and no-show ratio. You may identify others you want to track.

The information for your KPI will come from your accounting software. It takes time and effort to track this data and some people simply will not do it. Counselors and social workers in general seem to not be as focused on business numbers in my experience. I recommend that at a minimum, pay attention to the income statement.

Some definitions are probably in order:

Balance sheet - a snapshot at any given moment of a company's assets, liabilities, and equity. It gives an overview of whether the business is succeeding or failing. Your accounting software can create this report.

Income statement - also known as a profit and loss statement; shows financial performance over a given period. It neatly summarizes your income, expenses, and net profit after all bills are paid. It is probably the most important document. Look at it each month to determine how well your business is doing. Your accounting software should easily provide this for you.

Gross profit - Gross profit is the same as gross revenue for a service business. It is the amount of money coming in before anything is taken out to pay bills, etc.

Direct costs - the costs that can be traced back to specific activities, including labor, materials, or travel.

Indirect costs - costs that support your services, including rent, utilities, and marketing. Whether you see any clients or not, you will still incur these expenses.

Cost of services - I find this difficult to determine. If you made a product, you would add up the dollar amount of the materials it took to make it, plus how much you would pay someone to create the product. This is known as the cost of goods sold (COGS). For a service business like counseling, we determine the cost of services in a similar way except we are the product (our skills and knowledge). You can find out what your costs are for the month by looking at your accounting software and finding the average cost per client (costs/number of clients). This does not take into account your pay, however. Our pay at our office is not set up as an hourly wage or salary but is dependent on how much we bring in, which varies every month. The average cost per client would give you an idea of how much is left before being paid for your services. To plug in some numbers, if your costs are $2500 a month and you saw 100 clients, the average would be 2500/100 = $25 per client before you are paid. If insurance paid you $65, that would leave $40 for your pay minus some left over for business expenses (you wouldn't want to leave nothing in your bank account I hope). Costs of services do not contain indirect costs that do not contribute directly to providing the service.

Average revenue per session - the average amount of money you receive from clients and insurance per visit. My practice management software, MyClientsPlus, provides me with this report. The formula is revenue / # of clients. If your software does not calculate this, simply find how much revenue you brought in and count how many clients you saw that period to divide it with.

No-show ratio - the number of clients who failed to keep their appointment compared to the number of appointments. The formula is # no-show clients / total # of appointments. You would need to define whether to consider only those who truly failed to keep their appointments or also those who rescheduled.

Service or operating margin - the amount of profit you make before interest and taxes (EBIT in accounting talk). The formula is total revenue - total expenses.

Service profit margin - the ratio of net profits per dollar of revenue. The formula is net profit margin = (revenue - expenses) / revenue. To use our data, (65-25) / 65 = 62% or $40 per session.

Average cost per session - the sum of fixed (payroll and other costs of business whether you see clients or not) plus variable costs (advertising, temporary costs) per visit

Service revenue growth rate - the change in revenues from one period to another, can be measured in months, quarters, or years. Find the revenue for a particular period and compare it to another period. This might be helpful to follow to make sure your revenue is not getting eaten up by increasing expenses.

Start-up tip:

- You don't have to be a financial wizard to manage your business but having a general knowledge of these terms and watching your data can inform you on your progress.

Interoffice communication

In our old office, we had the luxury of being able to hear one another speaking without leaving our office. The client's waiting area was separate and behind a closed door.

In our new office space, the sound seems to travel easily between different businesses and down the hallway but not so much to a coworker in the next room. The acoustics were strange and we worked hard to protect client confidentiality, making it even more challenging to hear one another.

Of course, we could easily get up from our desks and go to another office to discuss something. We could also use our cell phones to call the other office. To save money, our office just has one traditional phone line. We do use cell phones sometimes to call clients for teletherapy.

After trying out several options, I tried Skype to send interoffice messages to one another. Again, we could use a cell phone to send messages but I keep mine on airplane mode so I am not interrupted during a session. I often don't look at it until the middle or end of the day.

I do, however, look at my computer every hour to check appointments, make new appointments, and do billing. Skype changes color to let me know I have a message waiting. You can also do group messages. You may find a different solution that works best for you. We tried Skype in the beginning but no longer use it now. It seems we adjusted to the new workspace and just did not need it as much.

Microsoft Teams seems like overkill for our needs. We just need to simply give each other messages, often when that person is not immediately available. There are some other chat options available. You might settle on a more simple, old-school solution (Post-it notes, message boards, etc.).

Start-up Tips:

- Try out different solutions and choose the ones that work best for you. Keep costs in mind when starting. There are many free options.

- The easiest option is usually the one you will use most.

Therapeutic Milieu

I always wanted a television for my office. For some reason, it made me feel I had finally made it. I was never able to have a television before I was in private practice so I decided now was the time to get one. My clients have enjoyed being able to watch soothing videos of underwater sea turtles and fish swimming around or different pictures of animals and nature. They find it very relaxing. I connected the television to the internet so I could stream videos from sites such as YouTube. I keep the sound very low so my client and I can talk. Another possibility is to utilize the connection between my computer and TV to watch brief therapeutic videos.

Most clients who seek counseling are trying to cope with depression and anxiety. Research has demonstrated that being in nature is restorative and therapeutic for all of us, even if it is just a picture. Nothing can replace the real thing but a television showing outdoor scenes is second best. I have never gone so far as to measure their pulse or blood pressure but it would be interesting to do so. Offices in the past had aquariums for the same reason but, a television is much easier to maintain and can be changed in an instant to something different.

When clients are not in my office, I sometimes watch training videos or listen to relaxing music. It's nice to be able to have the autonomy and independence to make your own decisions. During Christmas, it was especially nice to watch and listen to Christmas music. The Yule log made my office space feel warmer and cozier!

Start-up Tips:

- As a mental health provider, you most likely will already think about some ways to make your office inviting and safe. Go with what you like.
- Not only can you make your office attractive, but you can also use your knowledge of psychology to make it therapeutic!

5 CONCLUSIONS

After more than a year in private practice, I look back and ask myself, "Would I do that all over again?" The short answer is, yes, but probably make some different choices. To be more specific, I am very pleased about opening a private practice with my partner. It is rewarding to be a business owner where I have a say in what happens and have the ability to help others as I envisioned after finishing college. I don't have to follow some of the rules and regulations of other businesses that made no sense to me. I can make my schedule without having to ask anyone.

Overall, it has been a great experience. There are many things about opening a business I have learned. I had looked into opening businesses before but never got to the point of actually doing it.

What are the main lessons I have learned?

1.   An S Corp may not have been the best option for us after all.

a.   Required employees and payroll versus independent contractors. We knew we would become employees/owners and our part-time secretary would become an employee as well. We knew that entailed setting up our accounting system differently and we would be required to pay taxes. We did not expect to be so confused about how to go about it. It was much simpler with the partnership to have independent contractors who had to file their own taxes and needed little from the company. We finally were in contact with a QuickBooks trainer who provided us with advice and explanations on how to set up our accounts accurately. Even though we had used QuickBooks for years, the difference between a partnership and S Corp was significant. The first accountant, who did not work out for us, only provided a one-page list of accounts to set up, with no explanation or personalization. At least she did connect us with the local QuickBooks expert.

b.   The expense of payroll, quarterly taxes, more expensive associations with attorneys and accountants, and tax preparation were 3x what a partnership was. Payroll expenses for our three employees were surprisingly high just to have the software calculate the payroll and for the secretary to write out a check. With the partnership, there were no monthly payroll expenses. The secretary simply calculated everything by hand, which was fairly simple, and wrote a check by hand. Quarterly taxes now are tracked by the software, which isn't as simple as it sounds, and must be paid quarterly by the company to the state and IRS. It feels like there is more to track and keep up with. As a contractor, I simply calculated my expected annual income, divided it by four, and went on the IRS website where I set up automatic payments for the whole year. It was a one-time task each year. I did have to watch to make sure there was enough in my personal bank account to cover it quarterly but that also just involved a one-time reminder set-up.

Attorney fees cost us thousands of dollars for the initial setup of our business. I don't regret that, but attorneys were not as important in setting up a partnership. I do, however, recommend you have an attorney draft or look over your partnership agreement to avoid any potential conflict in how the business is run if you choose that route. Having this done up front is akin to having insurance, in my mind. It seems like you are paying a lot of money for little if any benefit but it is nice to have it when you need it.

I also think, in retrospect, it might have been easier and cheaper to choose one of those online businesses that charge a fee to file all the legal documents for you. If you are super-cautious and want personal guidance, then choose a local attorney over an online one. These online businesses often have access to an attorney for a fee but my research indicated many were not happy with the service they got. The attorneys were not as accessible or helpful as people wanted.

As for tax preparation, it costs us about 3x to do the taxes of an S Corp over a partnership. The partnership did not include the personal taxes of each partner, just the business itself. And that was the most reasonable offer. Some quoted even higher amounts. I was very satisfied with the services we got from the final accountant we chose, but did not realize at the onset just how expensive it could be.

2.   An S Corp did not save us hardly any money like we initially thought it would.

Taxes, accountant, attorney, S Corp filing. We were told by the first accountant that an S Corp would be the way to go. I believe she based it on her own business, which was an S Corp, but most likely brought in much more revenue than a counseling office. It was explained we would save about

15% in taxes each year because about one-third of our income could go into a tax-free distribution account and be used for many beneficial things. While that is technically true, it appears new tax laws have made it much less appealing to be an S Corp. These laws were just changing when we were given that advice, so I can't completely blame that office. However, 15% of a low revenue-producing company is not the same as 15% of a higher revenue-producing company.

We initially were saving too much in the distribution account, thinking it would benefit us when we used it for items such as covering bonuses, expenses, etc. When tax time came, we were penalized for not providing an adequate salary versus distribution, ending in extra taxes. Many sources I consulted recommended taking 50% of income in salary and 50% from distributions but this is too high on the distribution portion, potentially triggering an IRS audit. You never want that. You have to set your salary at whatever is the average or median salary for your area and any money in the distribution is just gravy.

3.   An S Corp has a lot more complexity than some of the other business models.

a.   We spent a lot of time and effort trying to figure out how to benefit from distributions. We don't have a degree in business or finance, so we only had a minimal understanding of certain terms and what they meant for our business.

b.   Taxes are more complicated, as detailed above.

c.   Tracking expenses is harder to set up compared to partnership

d.   We had to remember to schedule the required annual board of directors' meetings and annual shareholder meetings that normally you would not think about. These are required and prove you are a corporation. We have found the board of directors meeting and our quarterly meetings to be very beneficial as it helps us keep on top of how our business is doing.

4.   It may benefit us in the long run when one of us has to leave the practice.

Having fairly clear paperwork outlining what will happen when someone who owns the business moves on will prevent future headaches; it made us think about it beforehand. It doesn't hurt to think ahead of time about the whole lifespan of your business. Younger clinicians may think they have years to worry about things of that nature but, like having a will or power of attorney, it is better to have one and not need it than to need it and not have it.

5.   The business may go on after one of us leaves.

The partnership ended because one of the two had to quit. That essentially ended the business since the remaining partner was financially unable to own it alone. It might have been different under different circumstances. In this case, the owners of the old business also owned the property. The partner who was no longer working would have been responsible for her half of the mortgage since they owned the property, even though she was unable to work to bring in the income to cover it.

6.   It is a good idea to talk to as many people as you can who know about the ancillary items you don't know about. This includes other private practices, financial institutions, attorneys, accountants, and any other professionals. Don't go on the advice of just one but ask around.

We thought we were well-advised when an accountant recommended the S Corp but there were many negative things about it we were not told. We did not know enough to ask the right questions. In our particular case, we felt pressured to move forward because the old business was dissolving and we would essentially be unemployed. That particular accountant also would not answer follow-up questions, giving us the brush-off by telling us to consult another person.

7.   You might want to get some experience in the counseling and social work field before jumping into private practice. That way, you are sure it is what you want to do and you have clearer expectations.

a.   This did not apply to us but, I can't imagine trying to go into private practice if I had little or no experience as a counselor. It helped tremendously to know the ins and outs of insurance, payment, billing, electronic health records, and all the other details.

b.   My education and, I imagine, your education as well, did not prepare me at all for the business side of counseling. There are some entrepreneurs online who are addressing this issue and I recommend you check them out. I have not personally used them but I believe it is a good idea.

6 ADDITIONAL RESOURCES

ACA

The American Counseling Association has resources for LPC and other counseling licenses. There is no section devoted to start-ups but there may occasionally be articles of interest.

APA

The American Psychological Association has an article or two on starting in private practice but this website is generally directed towards PhD level readers. There are many resources here to help with your practice.

Doxy.me

Since the start of the pandemic, we have used doxy.me for telehealth. One major advantage is it is free but there are often glitches during a session that might require you to change access.

Google is negatively regarded by some due to personal privacy concerns but I happen to embrace Google as a way for clients to locate our new business. It offers helpful information with phone number, directions and a picture of our building. One of the better features I like is the monthly reporting I can receive, informing me how many visitors looked us up and what search terms they used. This is free, valuable information for optimizing your website if you have one. You can track trends related to your business, as well. One suggestion, you might want to check your business information and personal name to ensure the information is correct. I discovered our phone number was incorrect and people were unable to reach us if they called the number from the business profile. It was very easy to correct through Google.

Google docs

This website provides access to Google's free alternatives to Microsoft Office. I tend to use them frequently but occasionally have to save something in the .docx file extension for compatibility with other programs. I find it meets almost all of my needs for word processing and light spreadsheet functionality. Search Google for HIPAA compliance, and read and sign a business agreement to ensure you comply.

Google Reports

Google reports provide a wealth of information about how clients interact with Google to find your business. Type in "google my business" on Google search and it will direct you to your business profile. You can create, edit, and manage your profile from this page. Our profile report recently told us that 79% of people who search for our office use the mobile version and 26% searched for "cbt." You can use this to optimize your online presence on your business websites. It also provides the number of calls from the search and how many asked for directions. I added a photo of the outside of our office.

Google Voice

I obtained a free Google Voice number so I could make phone calls and text clients without giving out my personal phone number. There have been occasional glitches in call quality but I like the privacy it provides. Google Business starter package is only $8 per user per month and provides more features. Since I don't have as many telehealth sessions as I did during the pandemic, the basic free plan is all I need. Read and sign the business agreement with Google to ensure HIPAA compliance.

Google Workspace

If you are into the Google universe, you might consider Google Workspace. It provides online meeting space, email included, and the ability to save your documents to Google Drive. Check their business agreement and sign it to ensure it is HIPAA-compliant regarding sensitive, private information. I use it for forms, documents, and spreadsheets that do not include client data. They have a HIPAA Implementation Guide you can use.

Gusto

Gusto starts at $40 per month plus $6 per person for payroll automation. They also can help with onboarding new hires, time and attendance, and employee benefits. We did not look into this as we chose QuickBooks Payroll as our solution, but I wanted you to be aware of this option.

Heard.com

I only recently discovered this website but it has valuable information regarding bookkeeping and finances for any business. What makes it special, is it was designed by the accountant husband for his therapist wife. They saw a niche and filled it.

"How to Run an S Corporation" book

When researching just what an S Corp is and how to run one, I purchased this book, How to Start and Run Your Own Corporation: S Corporations for Small Business Owners, from Amazon. The author, Peter Hupalo, does a great job explaining the details and provides multiple examples that are easy to understand.

The Insurance Maze

Barbara Griswold is a fellow therapist who bravely tackles the insurance monster to explain things to us in easy-to-understand terms. She stays on top of changes in the industry. Ms. Griswold has informational videos, articles, continuing education credits, and many useful resources.

IRS

Yes, those people. The IRS does have useful information for starting your business but you must know what to search for. Allow your accountant to do most of this work but it helps to be knowledgeable about taxes that apply to your situation.

Kanbanflow

Kanban is a tool for identifying, organizing, and delegating tasks that need to be done as you work on getting your business off the ground. We found the online version, listed above, most useful as it allowed any of us to access it from the internet. It is collaborative and allows you to color code items of importance. Best of all, it is free for the basic version, which provided us with all we needed.

MyClientsPlus

When reading reviews of electronic health record companies, MyClientsPlus is not often listed. Our office has used them for years and we have been happy with their service, website uptime, and pricing. They were bought by therapybrands.com and aggregated with other EHR providers.

NASW

I did not find any articles about starting a private practice but it may be worthwhile to become a member for other reasons. They offer information on therapy and have access to discounts on insurance, and other benefits.

Office online

Office is, of course, the go-to business application. Many small businesses though may not be able to afford the whole package. Microsoft has provided other options. Windows includes free apps in the app store of Word, Excel, PowerPoint, and others. These are limited but generally, all that is needed for a small private practice. If you are still in college and have access to a student email, there is a free full version of Office on their website. Newer options include the sidebar on the Edge browser and sidebar extensions you can download for Chrome and Firefox. I like the easy access of these apps built into my browser since I typically use my browser most of the time.

Person-Centered Tech (PCT)

PCT is an extremely useful website when it comes to HIPAA compliance, a topic most therapists and social workers are uncomfortable with or don't want to expend effort on finding the most up-to-date information. They provide continuing education on these topics and materials to support your business.

"Private Practice Preparedness" book

This is a book by A. M. Wheeler and R. Reinhardt regarding the closing of a private practice due to retirement, death, or disability. You may ask why you would be interested in such a book at the start of your business but developing an exit strategy needs to be part of your business plan. It includes templates for any need you may have on this topic.

Psychology Today

Psychology Today provides individual pages for counselors to advertise themselves. Most of our referrals come from this source. If you have an account, you have free access to Sessions, an online telehealth service. It seems to work well but, clients are required to download an app to use it.

Psychotherapy Networker

This trade magazine is my favorite source for keeping up with topics relevant to the mental health field. It fits nicely in that space between consumer pop psychology and dry mental health journals. You can even earn continuing education credit for reading it.

QuickBooks

QuickBooks has always been the primary software for business accounting. There are others but we have been using the desktop version of QuickBooks in our office. It is complex and required us to get some outside help from a QuickBooks pro and our accountant to ensure we had everything set up properly.

S Corporations Explained

This is an excellent website run by an attorney. It should answer most of your questions and offers to set up your S Corp for you if you choose.

Wave Accounting

Per their website, Wave offers a suite of money tools to help you create invoices, accept payments, track expenses, and pay your staff. You can also get coaching from bookkeeping, accounting, and payroll experts. The accounting software is free.

Weebly.com

Weebly is a competitor of Wix and was the first one I used with the old business. It is a capable and easy-to-use place for website creation. Wix has more options if you plan on selling items on your website but Weebly is good for the basics. If you decide to make a business website, be sure to enable the phone app settings as most people will use their cell phone to find you.

Wix.com

Wix is one of the best places to create your business website. The tools are relatively easy to use and they can provide you with a domain name and hosting. The downside is they tend to be somewhat pricier than other website-building platforms. Enable the phone app settings so potential clients can search for you on their cell phones and find your website.

Youtube

Everyone knows about YouTube. The reason I have listed it here is I found many helpful videos on areas I felt weak in regards to starting a business. I watched videos to understand differences in business types, how to set up and use QuickBooks for an S Corp, and many other topics.

7 APPENDICES

Appendix A

Comparison Table for EHR companies

Attribute	Company A	Company B	Company C
Price	_____	_____	_____
Ease of Use	_____	_____	_____
Progress note Integration	_____	_____	_____
Navigation	_____	_____	_____
Electronic billing	_____	_____	_____
Appt reminders	_____	_____	_____
Calendar	_____	_____	_____
Credit card integration	_____	_____	_____
ERA	_____	_____	_____
Client portal	_____	_____	_____
_____	_____	_____	_____
_____	_____	_____	_____

Use whatever method works best for you to compare. I might give certain aspects stars, check marks, or input a number.

Appendix B

Insurance Provider List for Credentialing

There are hundreds, if not thousands, of insurance companies with which you could do business. I found one list with over 2,000 companies on it. The following is a list of the major ones you might consider. Ask colleagues what insurances they take, which ones are easiest to do business with, and which ones are not.

Insurance Company	Counselor	Group
Aetna	_____	_____
Anthem	_____	_____
BCBS	_____	_____
BeaconHealth	_____	_____
ChampUS	_____	_____
Cigna/Evernorth	_____	_____
HCSC	_____	_____
Humana	_____	_____
Kaiser Permanente	_____	_____
Magellan	_____	_____
MCA	_____	_____
Medicaid	_____	_____
Medicare	_____	_____

Military OneSource	_____	_____
Molina Health	_____	_____
OneHealthcare (Optum, UHC, UMR)	_____	_____
TriCare	_____	_____
United Health	_____	_____
ValueOptions	_____	_____
Wellpoint	_____	_____

If you are starting fresh in the counseling or social work business, it might be fruitful to do some research about what insurance companies provide mental health benefits in your state. If you are credentialed in more than one state, you would want to check those as well. I have included the largest insurance providers in the country in the table but some may not be offered where you live.

You may want to be credentialed as an individual but also as a group. The rules differ by insurance company. If you own the business, it would be ideal to credential the group, making it easier to onboard new counselors later on under the group credential.

The information I included on this table when I was engaged in the credentialing process is the dates of acceptance per the contract and/or acceptance letter, the date I could do electronic billing, and a provider number if provided. That way, any time you need to contact an insurance company, this information is readily accessible. We also keep an index card with our basic information on it: provider numbers for each insurance company, our tax ID, NPI, and any other information we need when calling an insurance company.

Appendix C

Start-Up Budget

A start-up budget is different from your regular monthly budget. You will want to think about the initial costs of opening a business. These are usually one-time expenses or occasional purchases as you grow or replace outdated and broken items. You might not need or want all of these items but they are listed in the table as a reminder of what you might need to purchase.

ITEM	COST
Computer equipment/printers	_____
Copier	_____
Fax machine	_____
Telephone system	_____
Business mobile phones	_____
Staff furniture (desks, chairs, tables, and bookshelves)	_____
Client furniture	_____
Office accessories and decorations	_____
Lighting	_____
Office supplies (paper, pens, staplers, Ink, paper clips, etc.)	_____
Deposits on location/utilities	_____
Installation fees for services (internet, WIFI, Telephone, networking)	_____
Painting and preparation of space	_____
Business start-up filing fees (federal, state, And local)	_____

Attorney consultation fees   _____

Accountant consultation fees   _____

Signage   _____

Logo/letterhead   _____

Other   _____

TOTAL   _____

Appendix D

Example Budget

You will want to start developing a budget as early as possible. I started out thinking there would not be that much overhead for a counseling business. It doesn't require lots of equipment and I am selling my knowledge and skills, not a physical product. Once you realize all the requirements and small things that are needed, the budget grows. Keeping expenses to a minimum and maximizing your income will lead to profitability.

I suggest you print out this budget sheet and fill in the information as you narrow things down. Some items may only be an annual cost. I kept things like this in a physical notebook as that worked best for me. You might do better with a digital version. The more adventurous might even create a spreadsheet to automatically update as you go.

ITEM	MONTHLY	ANNUALLY
Rent	_____	_____
Electricity, if not included	_____	_____
Water	_____	_____
Gas	_____	_____
Trash and/or shredding	_____	_____
Internet access	_____	_____
Telephone (landline)	_____	_____
Mobile phones	_____	_____

HIPAA-compliant email _____ ⁄ _____

Electronic health record/billing _____ _____

Malpractice insurance _____ _____

Liability insurance _____ _____

Website hosting/domain _____ _____

Office supplies (pens, paper, etc. _____ _____

Software (accounting,
    word processing,
     antivirus, backup,
     password mgr) _____ _____

Marketing (business cards,
    ads, social media) _____ _____

Fees (Federal, state, and local) _____ _____

Licensure renewal _____ _____

Continuing education _____ _____

Organizational dues _____ _____

Accounting fees _____ _____

Housekeeping/cleaning _____ _____

Miscellaneous _____ _____

TOTAL _____ _____

Whew! That's a lot of expenses. And we haven't even mentioned getting paid somewhere along the way. Don't let all the expenses overwhelm you. Thousands of counselors are in private practice and make it work. You can too. My goal is to inform you so there are no surprises. Again, managing your expenses is the key to profitability.

Suggested Roadmap

You may disagree with the order of some items. Use this as a general guideline as you plan your business.

1.   You have an idea to go into private practice; consider the pros and cons list from this book and add your own. This book assumes you already are licensed to practice in your state. If not yet licensed, you might want to consider focusing on that first, unless going into business with someone who is licensed.

2.   Clarify your target customer and determine your niche, consider complementing one another's skills in your office if you have more than one counselor. Decide how many counselors will go into private practice together and define their role. Start creating a business plan outline with all these details.

3.   Identify your stakeholder categories - clients, owners, independent contractors, employees, and vendors. Vendors are any person or company who supplies a service or product to help you with your business. Create a list of companies you might want to work with.

4.   Create a flexible schedule for your project using a calendar or Kanban.

5.   Choose a business and tax structure; e.g., partnership, etc. Think about the possibility of expansion later, both from a business standpoint and office space.

6.   Create a business plan - types of therapy, clients, cash vs. insurance, SWOT, goals, and budget. Do your own plan. Develop an exit strategy and

do the work ahead of time when everyone is on good terms. Find your estimated breakeven point.

7. Once you have decided on a business structure, contact your state and local business websites for forms. Make a calendar of when to file certain forms, and how much they cost, and consider printing out paper copies of electronic forms for your records.

8. Contact local government websites and offices to comply with local ordinances, taxes, etc.

9. Scout out locations fairly early. Match locations to your research on the ideal client and where they can easily access your office if you have a physical location for in-person care. Accessibility should include convenience but also include handicapped accessibility with available parking.

10. Identify what services you need assistance with in your business operations (such as accountant, attorney, etc.) and get estimates for services.

11. Identify local contacts for taxes, legal, banking, rental property, insurance coverage, utilities, internet access, advertising (social media?), signage, SBA, and SCORE.

12. Hire attorneys, accountants, insurance companies, and other pertinent support.

13. Establish the business by filing forms, etc. Register and obtain a TIN (tax identification number) or EIN (employee identification number if you are a sole proprietor or independent contractor) from your state government.

14. Create a business manual and a corporation book that contains articles of incorporation, stock information, and other pertinent information if you have chosen S Corp as your business structure. If you have chosen another structure, it is still advisable to create a business manual where you outline policies, procedures, and other information on running your business.

15. Obtain location, sign a lease, and get utilities connected if necessary. Consider room to add therapists if desired. Is it scalable and would you want to expand?

16. Prepare the office space by completing any renovations. Create a safe, inviting atmosphere for your clients. We were able to save lots of money by bargain-hunting. A glass and metal desk was purchased for only $5 at an estate sale.

17. Set a move-in date and schedule with a mover if needed.

18. Purchase any needed materials - furniture, computers and software (accounting, Microsoft Office, EHR), phones, office supplies, and HIPAA compliance materials. Open a business bank account. This item is further down the list than you might expect. The reason for this is we could not open a bank account without having a registered business with the state and a mailing address for the business.

19. Start insurance panel credentialing of providers. This is also further down the list because of the need for bank accounts, permanent mailing addresses, etc. You could start on this earlier and not send it until you have all the information.

20. Develop an online presence with Psychology Today, Google, local websites, a company website, email, LinkedIn, or others.

21. Consider joining local mental health networking groups to get the word out about your new business and to get referrals if needed. There are state-level and local-level meetings for both social workers and licensed professional counselors in my state. These groups meet in person and stay connected through Facebook and other online sites. Start letting others know of your opening date.

22. Set up EHR and choose a credit card processing company.

23. Begin seeing clients once you are on insurance panels or sooner if you take self-pay clients.

24. Put important dates on your calendar regarding payment of taxes, refiling of fees, and other items that are not a regular part of business and could be overlooked.

25. Establish monthly meetings about progress toward business plan goals. Constant meetings are a drain on productivity but are useful at the beginning of your business start-up. We now have quarterly meetings. You would think we accomplish all that is needed by day-to-day business interactions but monthly or quarterly meetings bring a higher-level outlook to things. We look at monthly client visits, income, business needs, and other items we don't think about daily.

26. Set up data tracking tools that measure things such as number of clients seen each month, income, expenses, and other important things you want to track. Watching these items monthly will help identify both good and bad trends for your business so you can make informed decisions.

27. Establish quarterly officer and shareholders meetings if S Corp is chosen. Put a reminder on the calendar to have the required annual corporate and shareholders meetings, if applicable.

28. Pay quarterly taxes and other fees.

29. Review and tweak your business plan regularly. Re-evaluate and correct any procedures that are not efficient or working as you had thought at the beginning when they were chosen.

INDEX

ABOUT THE AUTHOR

Harold Leonard, M.A., LPC-MHSP has been working in the mental health field since 1988. He was first licensed in Tennessee in 1991 as a senior psychological examiner and in 2006 switched to a licensed professional counselor.

Over the years, he has worked in community mental health, inpatient psychiatric care, partial hospitalization, intensive outpatient, and private practice. He has been working in private practice since 2009.

All of these opportunities have resulted in him not only working with incredible people but also learning many things along the way that helped him with his current endeavor.

Do you have any suggestions or input? Are there things you would have included in this book that are not included? Are there things you want to know about in more detail?

You may contact the author at hleonard@centurylink.net.

www.ingramcontent.com/pod-product-compliance
Lightning Source LLC
Chambersburg PA
CBHW072213290526
45794CB00004B/1743